Kunsthalle Bega Box

Kunsthalle Bega is an alternative and experimental art space founded in 2019 at Timișoara by Alina Cristescu, Liviana Dan and Bogdan Rața through the Calina Foundation. Dedicated to supporting artistic production and understanding the current problems of the creative spectrum from a curatorial perspective, it awards the Bega Art Prize* to a Romanian curator who manages to change curatorial perception. Involved in educational projects with diverse communities, Kunsthalle Bega promotes the significant importance of art publications.

Kunsthalle Bega este un spațiu alternativ și experimental de artă, fondat în 2019 la Timișoara de Alina Cristescu, Liviana Dan și Bogdan Rața prin Fundația Calina. Dedicată susținerii producției artistice și înțelegerii problemelor actuale ale spectrului creativ din perspectivă curatorială, acordă premiul Bega Art Prize* unui curator român care reușește să schimbe regulile percepției actului curatorial. Implicată în proiecte educaționale cu comunități diverse, promovează importanța majoră/ vitală a publicațiilor de artă.

** Diana Marincu (2022), Cosmin Costinaș (2021), Sandra Demetrescu (2020), Anca Verona Mihuleț (2019)

Team / Echipa
Andreea Băban, Vlad Cîndea, Alina Cristescu, Liviana Dan, Andreea Drăghicescu, Loredana Ilie, Bogdan Rața, Andreea Tiriplică, Ugron Lajos

Kunsthalle Bega Box

KERBER ART

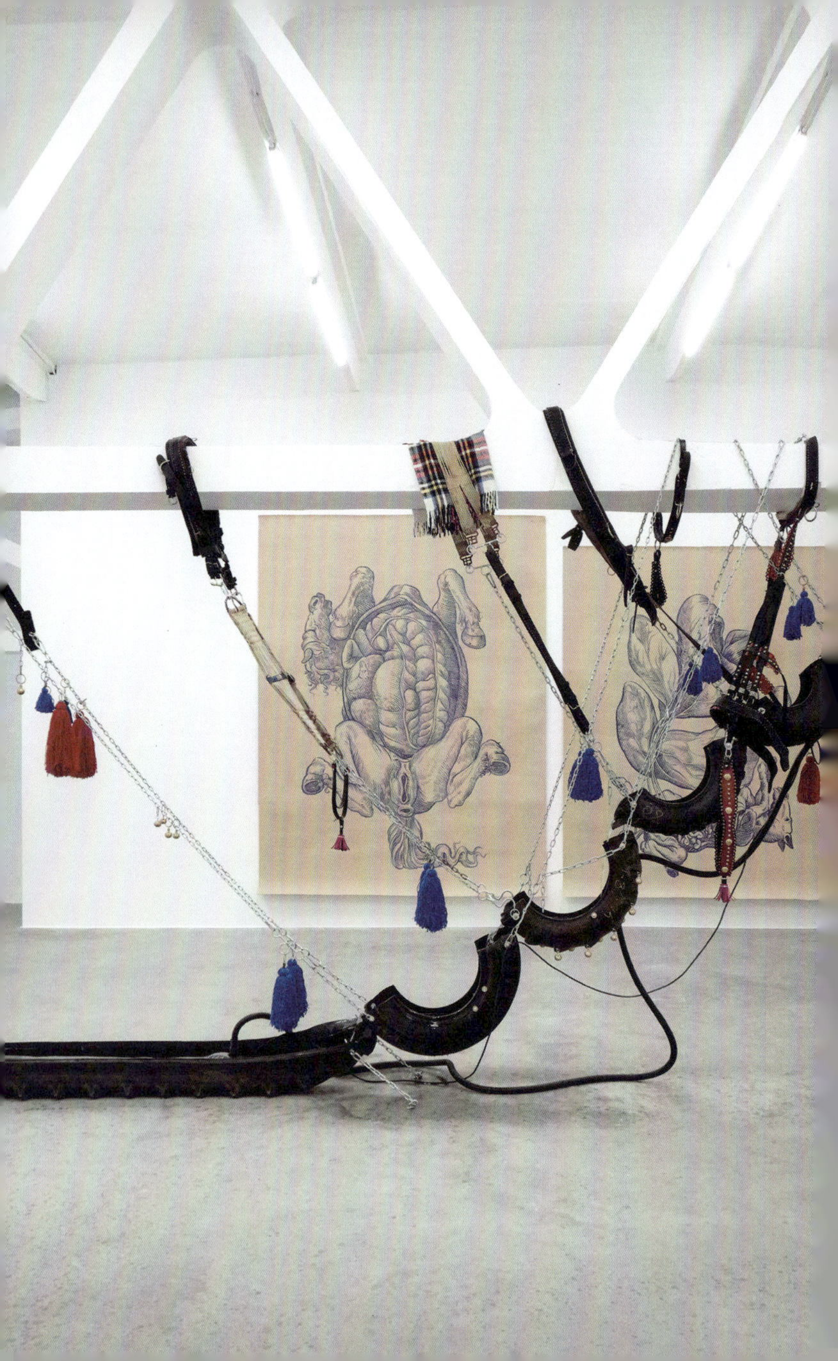

Contents

L' Anatomia del Cavallo, Dan Vezentan
exhibition view, 2021
previous page

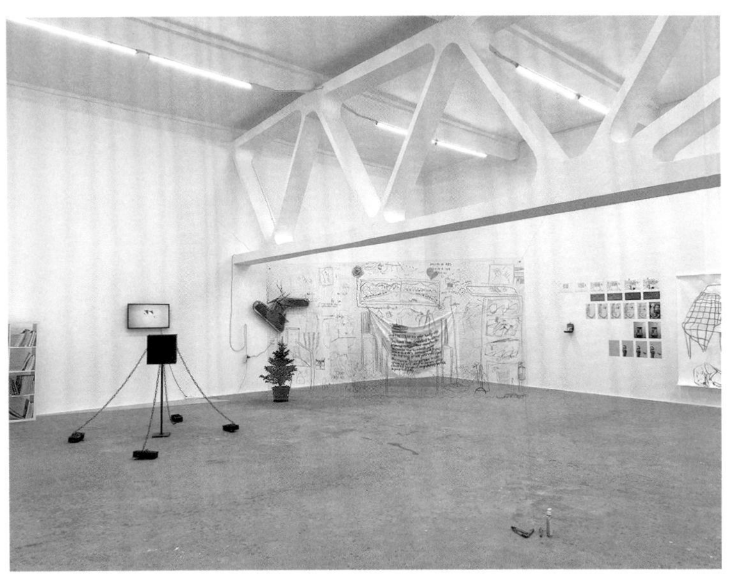

Later Edit
exhibition view, 2020

The Plan
Anca Verona Mihuleț

The way we perceive spaces of intersection and
interaction is determined by a conglobation of
elements, ranging from personal or collective sensory
practices to corporeal awareness and to psychological
factors; whether we are talking about the museum
or the gallery, the exhibition space pertains to the
category of spaces of intersection and interaction,
together with other forms of *loci*, like the department
store, as described by Walter Benjamin, or the street,
as described by the Situationists. The various modes
of displaying "things" are meant to concretize daily
or long-term experiences and render them in atypical
forms that would complicate perception, raise
questions, or attract the observer into an ontological
game.

The history of displaying art in a way that would
benefit both the beholder and the institution, while
offering a vibrant and contextual presentation of
the artists, dates back to the beginning of the 20th
century; notable and well-documented examples
come from Germany, where Hugo von Tschudi, first
as director of Nationalgalerie in Berlin and later of
the Neue Pinakothek in Munich, proposed alternative,
differentiated methods for showing French
Impressionists or German artists. During the Weimar
Republic, the activity of the group of thinkers and
practitioners around Bauhaus created a system for
representing all forms of art to the public in the most
functional and rational way possible – from specific
architectures to design strategies.

In 1939, at the 10th anniversary of the Museum of
Modern Art in New York, that coincided with the
inauguration of its new building designed by architect
Philip L. Goodwin, Alfred Barr curated the exhibition
Art in Our Time, which consisted of a democratic setting
of European and American art, showing paintings,
sculptures, prints, photographs, films, folk art and even
children's painting. It was a bold project that presented
"the Museum of Modern Art as a laboratory: in its
experiments the public is invited to participate."[1]
Laboratory – experiment – public – participation – so well
brought together in a statement at the end of Barr's
curatorial introduction in the catalogue of the exhibition,
although the arrangement of the artworks was considered
conservatory by some critics. But this quadruple stance
will become relevant for most exhibition organizers in
the next half of the century and beyond.

Charlotte Klonk, in her seminal book *Spaces of
Experience: Art Gallery Interiors from 1800 to 2000*, argues
that "the white cube never existed. It is true that
there were white walls in the art gallery – they were
introduced into German museums in the 1930s, taken
up by the Museum of Modern Art in New York and
spread to galleries all over the rest of the Western world
– but the object of giving museums their uniformly
white walls was never to create the enclosed space of
a cube. They were meant, rather, to produce a growing
and open space that would be flexible and adaptable."[2]

Adaptability, reconversion, and creative strategies are
characteristics of the emergence of art spaces in
post-revolutionary Romania. The initiatives and
projections of cultural agents and artists represent

the backdrop of the history of exhibition spaces that has been subjected to a more accelerated process compared to the less progressive regional cultural policies.

The Western city of Timișoara makes no exception. In 2019, the Kunsthalle Bega was inaugurated; its founders, Alina Cristescu, Liviana Dan and Bogdan Rața, started from the very idea that the white cube is a utopia and decided to convert a part of an iconic industrial building into a "Kunsthalle." The building is symbolic of Timișoara, as it was one of the locations where the first protests against the communist dictatorship took place in December 1989. The architectural style of the construction, finalized at the beginning of the 1950s, is quite intimidating and imposes an attitude – one must answer to the specific design of the building, it is impossible to ignore it.

An astute and timeless theorist of spaces, Siegfried Kracauer, famously asserted: "spatial images are the dreams of society. Wherever the hieroglyphics of these images can be deciphered, one finds the basis of social reality."[3] Kracauer identified two types of spatial images that need to be deciphered: firstly, there are the ones that are "consciously formed" and can be found in plans and guidebooks, and secondly, there are the ones considered to be "fortuitous creations" – configurations of buildings, streets, and figures which the individual confronts.[4] The Kunsthalle Bega falls into the second category. Layers of history and architectural details – the lighting system and the plugs are invisible in the space, thus emphasizing the primordial construction elements – together with traces of past exhibitions and projects, offer an entry point into the understanding of a city's narratives.

But the vast exhibition hall hides a metaphorical space – the Kunsthalle Bega Box – whose geometry informs punctual, smaller projects that often make a statement.

The Box is a distinct place, an appendix to the main hall, that can function as a traditional gallery when its walls are supporting drawings or paintings, as an expandable locus when it circumscribes installations, or as a projection room when it hosts video projections. The team behind Kunsthalle Bega situates itself at the intersection between visual arts, art history, journalism, and literature, and consequently there is a multidisciplinary approach to the projects and programmes hosted in the space.

Equinox, the first exhibition to be opened in the Kunsthalle Bega Box in 2020, showcased a series of paintings produced by Șerban Savu, under the curation of Mihai Pop, co-founder of the Plan B Gallery in Cluj. Initially conceived to be presented on the day of the spring equinox, the exhibition, which revolved around works carefully displayed at eye level, respecting the rhythm of the space, and privileging the viewer, communicated the shifting and often contradictory relation between humans, cities, and nature, while starting a conversation between light and darkness. Although the subject was not new, the innovation resided in the way Savu restored the faith in the pictorial dimension, demonstrating once again that there is a parallel world behind the surface tension provided by the canvas. Also, the exhibition conveyed a degree of intimacy and complicity between two old friends – Șerban Savu and Mihai Pop have been collaborators since the early 2000s.

The following project, *Later Edit,* curated by a local art historian specialized in post-communist Romanian art, Maria Orosan-Telea, gathered a group of young artists from Timișoara and Cluj and focused on the preparatory processes behind the artistic production. The project was one chapter of a broad curatorial research entitled *Draft,* which began in 2018. Orosan-Telea reflected on how a cumulus of ideas can be shaped by a collective over time and in unexpected contexts, also analyzing how commonly lived experiences were perceived by creators working across various media. The imposed distance and uncertainty derived from finalizing the project in the second wave of the pandemic tested the limits of the artist-curator collaboration and added a necessary strain to the experiment.

After a long career as a designer for Romanian avant-garde fashion labels like Rozalb de Mura and Patzaikin, Oláh Gyárfás dedicated himself to exploring form and materiality. The exhibition *Szénaizmok szalaghegyen / Haystacks on the Mountain of Ribbons* was conceived especially for the Box and takes its starting point in the exploration of local mythologies and beliefs. Drawing inspiration from the methods of Cy Twombly or Art Deco sculpture, Oláh created two imaginary creatures – Crocote and Leucrocote – whose names are borrowed from Pliny the Elder's *Naturalis Historia.* The two totems bear an accumulation of extraordinary features peculiar to domestic animals. The artist considered them personal friends and confidantes, protectors of unrealized ideas and suspended dreams.

The synthetic universe proposed by Laurian Popa, a young artist based in the city of Arad, famous for the cluster dedicated to the research of new media initiated by the collective Kinema Ikon, continued the series dedicated to painting. The alignment of large-scale works depicting everyday life objects that had been deprived of consistency to such a degree that they softened up, becoming fluid and spongy, was doubled by an animation that seemed to be a laboratory demonstration about the meaning of *Soft Objects*.

Dan Vezentan was the first artist to use the transversal beam separating the space in two, making it part of an installation – more specifically, the beam became the spine of an outsized horse whose shape was being suggested by cut out tires from a tractor, chains, harnesses, saddles, and tassels. This fantastic horse also served as a fountain for the spirits of the animals encapsulated in Vezentan's anatomical drawings, which, the artist imagined, were coming down at night to drink from that fountain. The exhibition was titled suggestively *L' Anatomia del Cavallo*, a tribute to this amazing animal that was "the engine" before the industrial revolution. The anatomical studies of horses take us back to late Renaissance and the debut of Mannerism, in an attempt of the artist to emphasize the irreversible social transformation.

Opposing Dan Vezentan's demonstration was Mihai Zgondoiu's project *The Approximate Man 3.0*. Zgondoiu recreated a Sci-Fi environment underpinning the traces of alien encounters, paranormal activities and out-of-this-world beings that coalesce in the pages of the artist's old sketch books and his collection of magazines. In the blue light, with the oblique desks holding catalogues of articles about extraterrestrial activities, the Box looks like a spaceship that is returning from a distant universe packed with discoveries. The artist stated that the project, which he has been working on over the last fifteen years, is not about the presentation of some striking art pieces or about offering answers, but rather about creating a different experience for the viewer who should leave loaded with questions.

The open format of the artistic discourse was adopted by the curatorial collective KILOBASE BUCHAREST for the parallel exhibitions *TRIUMF AMIRIA LOVE LETTER TO IRINA BUJOR / TRIUMF AMIRIA LOVE LETTER TO MIHAI MIHALCEA*, as part of the large-scale research project *TRIUMF AMIRIA*, dedicated to the first extensive institutional presentation of queer art produced in the past twenty years in Romania. The project, endorsed by the National Museum of Contemporary Art, was hosted by several institutions in Bucharest, before migrating to other locations in Europe, in the form of smaller artistic demonstrations. The two shows in the Kunsthalle Bega Box discuss the conflictual processes behind the formation of identity, putting in balance the impact of popular culture, performativity as a tool for fighting indifference or the disparities between reality and the imagined personal worlds.

In the last part of 2022, the Box was a meta-house during Ioana Maria Sisea's project *Harvest Time*. Over a period of four years, Sisea transformed all the objects in her grandparents' house into beads. Hundreds of strings loaded with beads made from diverse materials – glass, metal, paper, textile, wood – were hung from the ceiling, mimicking the configuration of the old house. It can be interpreted as a strategy for preserving personal history while contributing to coagulating a collective memory, and that is because the transformed objects were characteristic of a generation and a region.

In the past three years, the Kunsthalle Bega Box successively became a laboratory and experimental space for young and mid-career Romanian artists, showcasing comprehensive projects involving research and representation and engaging the audience in a phenomenological cultural experience. For the future, the members of the Kunsthalle Bega team aim to open the Box towards rediscussing and stressing the limits of materiality in conjunction with the performative display of new media.

editing / proofreading: Laura Balomiri

[1] Alfred Barr, "Art in Our Time. The Plan of the Exhibition," in the catalogue of the exhibition *Art in Our Time*, Museum of Modern Art, New York, 1939, p. 15.

[2] Charlotte Klonk, *Spaces of Experience: Art Gallery Interiors from 1800 to 2000*, University Press, Haven & London, 2009, p. 218.

[3] Apud *The Hieroglyphics of Space. Reading and experiencing the modern metropolis*, edited by Neil Leach, Routledge, London and New York, 2005, p. 143.

[4] Ibidem, p. 17.

TRIUMF AMIRIA LOVE LETTER TO IRINA BUJOR
exhibition view, 2022
next page

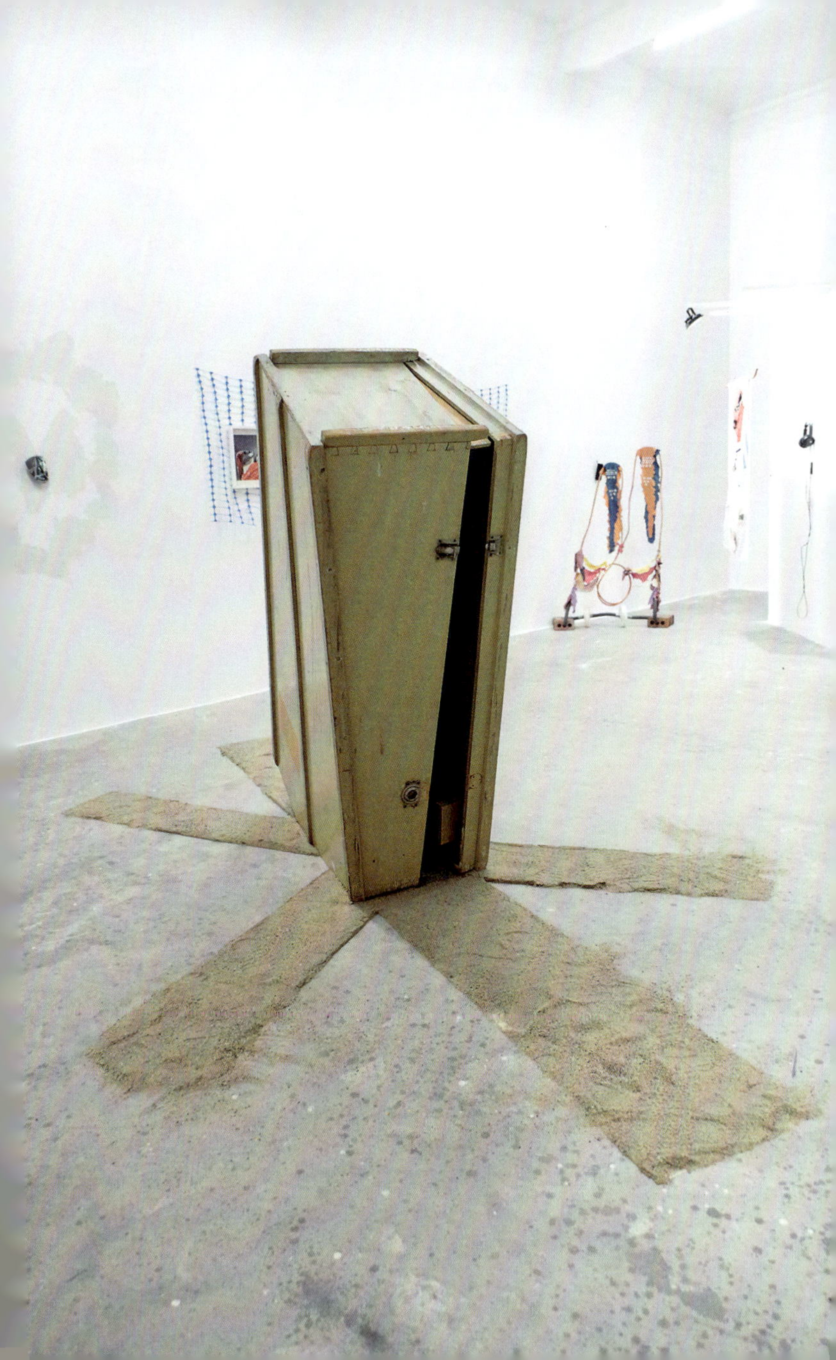

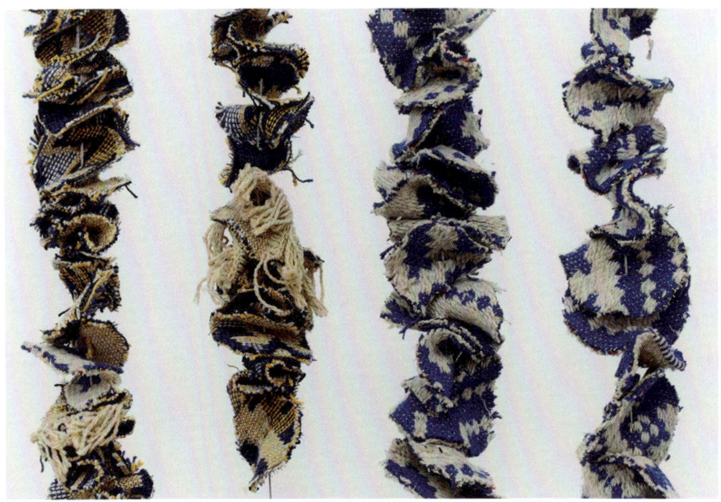

Harvest Time
installation
(detail)

Harvest Time
Ioana Maria Sisea

02. 09 – 16. 10. 2022
curators: Anca Verona Mihuleț, Iris Ordean

"My grandparents had a house, three beds, four tables,
fourteen chairs, twenty-seven glasses, forty-four
plates, three televisions, five carpets…
My grandparents lived in one of the four rooms of the
house; the other three were kept as a stage set that we
couldn't touch. They were *the good rooms* to which only
important people who came to visit, such as priests or
more distant relatives, had access."

This is a fragment of how Ioana Maria Sisea
remembers her maternal grandparents' house.
There are no traces of nostalgia to be found, but
we can speak about the responsibility implied by
memory that paves the way for an understanding
of the poetics of a space known in depth over a
long period of time, both from a material and
formal perspective. Memory becomes, thus, almost
a medium in itself, essential for its allegorical
potential in the installation's visual representation,
in organizing an account of aesthetic preoccupations.
With the death of her grandparents, Ioana's
relationship with the house in which she grew up
was transformed. The house itself became a spatial
construct loaded with layers of memory; stripped
of daily activities and the tension of the immediate,
the house was embedded in a distinctly contoured
personal geography. The absolute democratization of
space was necessary to save the memory of place.

The title of the exhibition, *Harvest Time*, is a
direct reference to the way in which in autumn,
in Mediterranean regions or in some areas of
Southeastern Europe, vegetables and fruit are often
dried on threads of string and then hung from
the ceiling beams or walls of houses. For Ioana,
this association has a special significance, being
a reference to the agricultural activities around
her grandparents' house, but also a tribute to the
processes that involve physical labour, both in art and
in daily life. The installation speaks of the intimacy
of lived memory through the magnifying glass. With
the metaphor of *harvesting*, we are granted access
to the artist's universe, informed by subjective past
experience. Socio-political memory makes way for
the installation of the reflexive memory codifying
art both cognitively and emotionally, through which
an abstracted archive emerges, a Derridean place of
commencement and commandment.

There are many ways in which we can document
private space – we can refer to the cosmological
formula proposed by Gaston Bachelard in *The Poetics
of Space*; or to the antagonism between pollution and
purification explored by Mary Douglas as early as the
1960s; or to the key structuralist interpretation offered
by Pierre Bourdieu in his study of Kabyle houses in
Algeria, based on binary dichotomies: woman – man,
inside – outside, birth – death; or more recently
to Griselda Pollock's or Jane Rendell's theories of
modernity and the gender of space.

Ioana has eliminated the borders imposed by walls
and meticulously, she started to register and index

all of the items which were found in her grandparents'
house at the moment it was inherited by the following
generation, room by room, item by item, material by
material. This activity turns the artist into a meditative
archivist, working from and with reflexive memory,
just like an agent. The disappearance of their users led
to the abstraction of those possessions. Traditional
documentation was continued by performative
actions that sought to divide all the objects in the
house into *beads* – glass and metal were melted and
reshaped into spherical shapes, wood was fretworked
into round elements, and textiles were hand-cut into
circles. Memory functions as a deconstructive and
reconstructive performative agent simultaneously –
two phenomena which are acting at the same time,
similarly to the principle of action – reaction. That
is to say, in addition to the immense affective labour
the artist put into creating the work for almost five
years, a more hands-on labour juxtaposes, one of literal
deconstruction: melting, cutting, drilling through,
adapting the working technique to the needs of each
material. A deconstruction, piece by piece, of the
former familial living and social habitus, as described
by Pierre Bourdieu and Zander Navarro, transforming
items which had formally contributed to the everyday
lived experience of which she was a part of very often
during her childhood: from chairs, beds, carpets, to
house appliances, invoices, cups and glasses. Elements
of everyday use sit together with *the Sunday clothes,*
or *the good cutlery.*

To it, a reconstructive approach closely follows: the
transformation of the contents of the grandparents'
house into beads, which is part of a spatial

progression and a re-production of meanings; the beads, typical of female representations, became the code for understanding the entire house. In this way, Ioana Maria Sisea identified her childhood home with an eminently feminine, mobile universe.

In the context of the first presentation of the project in the Kunsthalle Bega Box, strings of beads are placed side by side to create penetrable walls that depict the blueprint of the grandparents' house. Each bead wall is specific to a room, made from the divided objects that were once part of that room. Very few items survive the transformative process, testimonies of a former destiny anchoring the installation's past and present histories.

The film showing the gathering of objects and breaking down of the furniture, together with two photographs from the artist's childhood, are the only helpful elements that allow the audience to imagine the evolution of that *locus*, as if the viewer was watching through the keyhole, catching quick glimpses of a reality which is now transformed forever.

Anca Verona Mihuleț, Iris Ordean

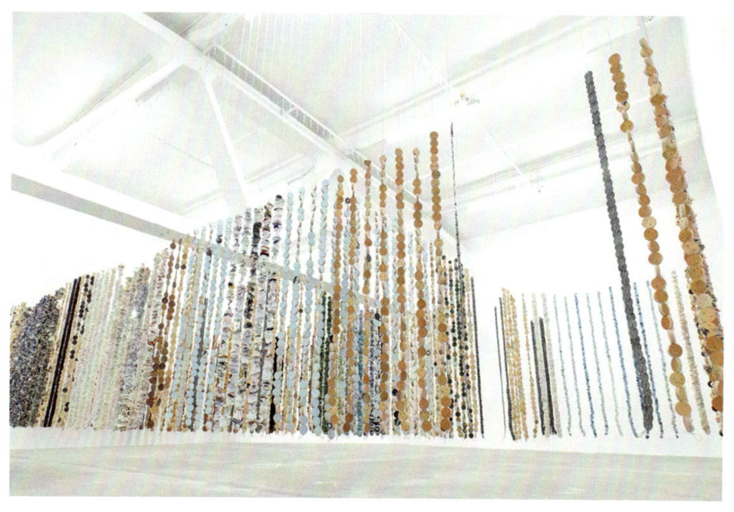

Harvest Time
installation view

Harvest Time
installation view

next spread

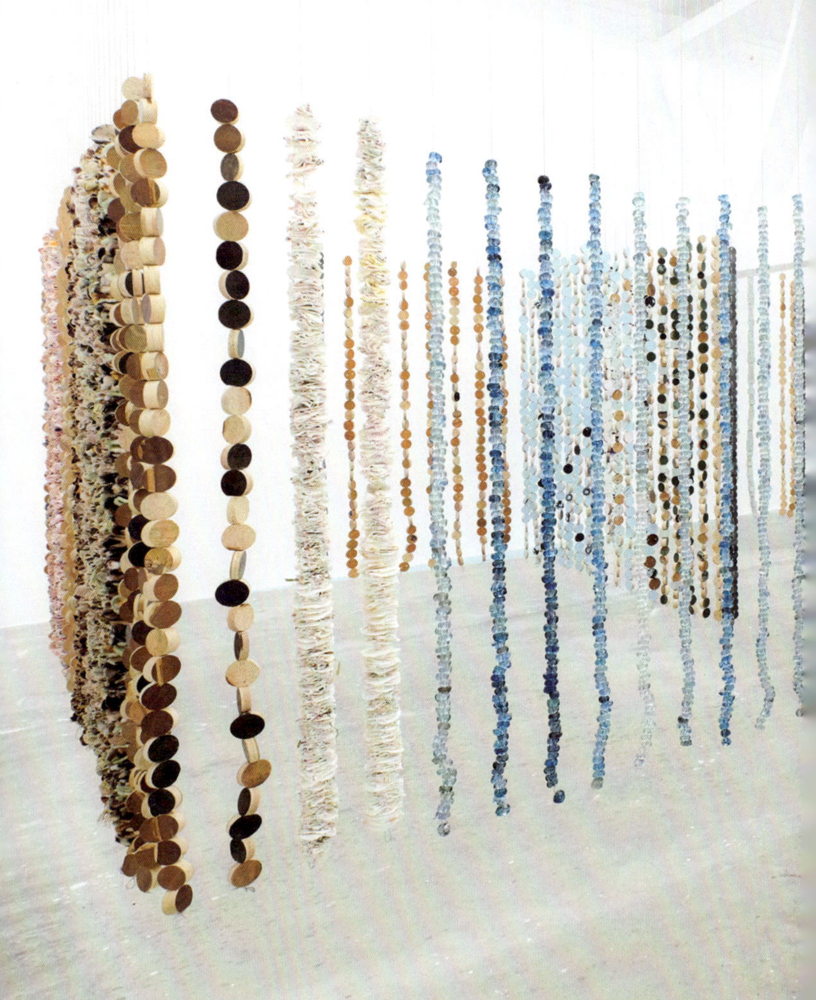

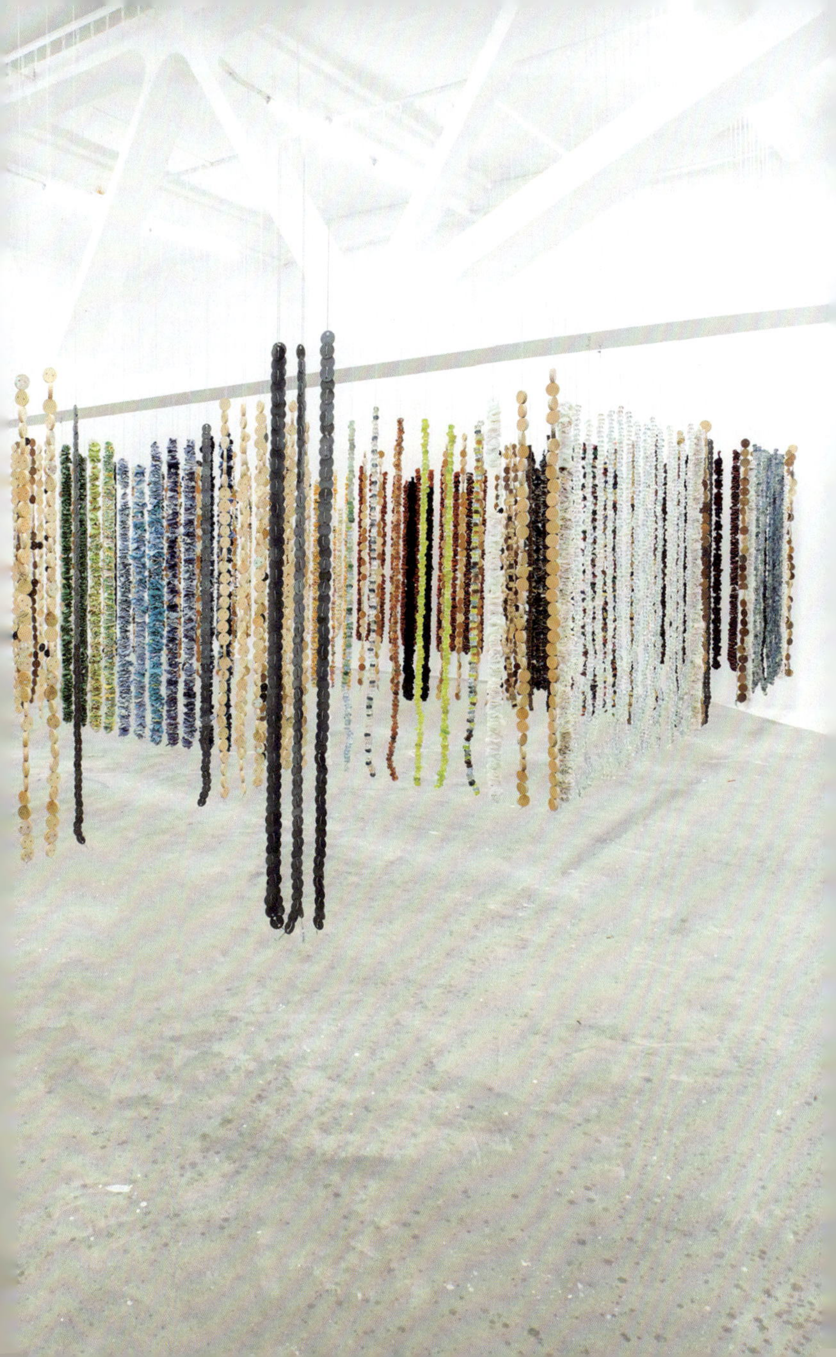

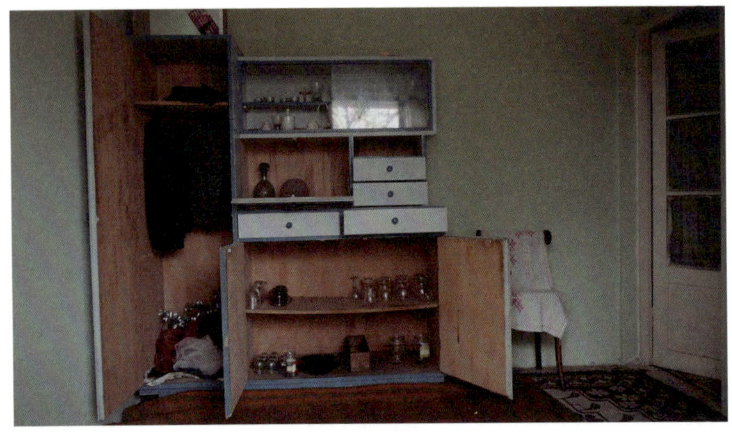

Still from the video documentation of the decomposition process taking place in the grandparents' house, produced by Ioana Maria Sisea in 2018

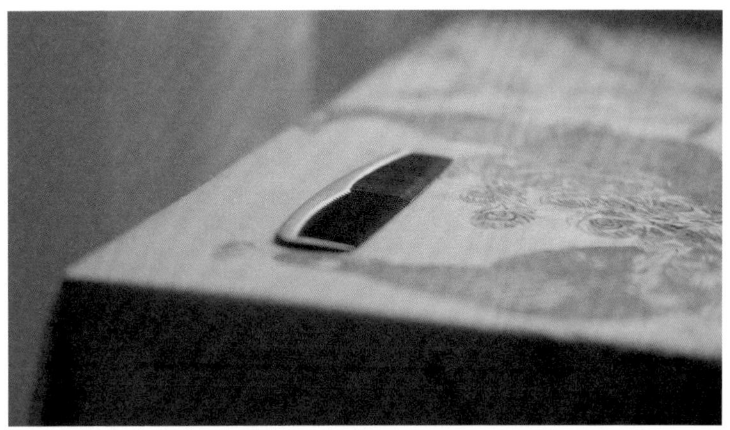

Still from the video documentation of the decomposition process taking place in the grandparents' house, produced by Ioana Maria Sisea in 2018

Harvest Time
installation view

next spread

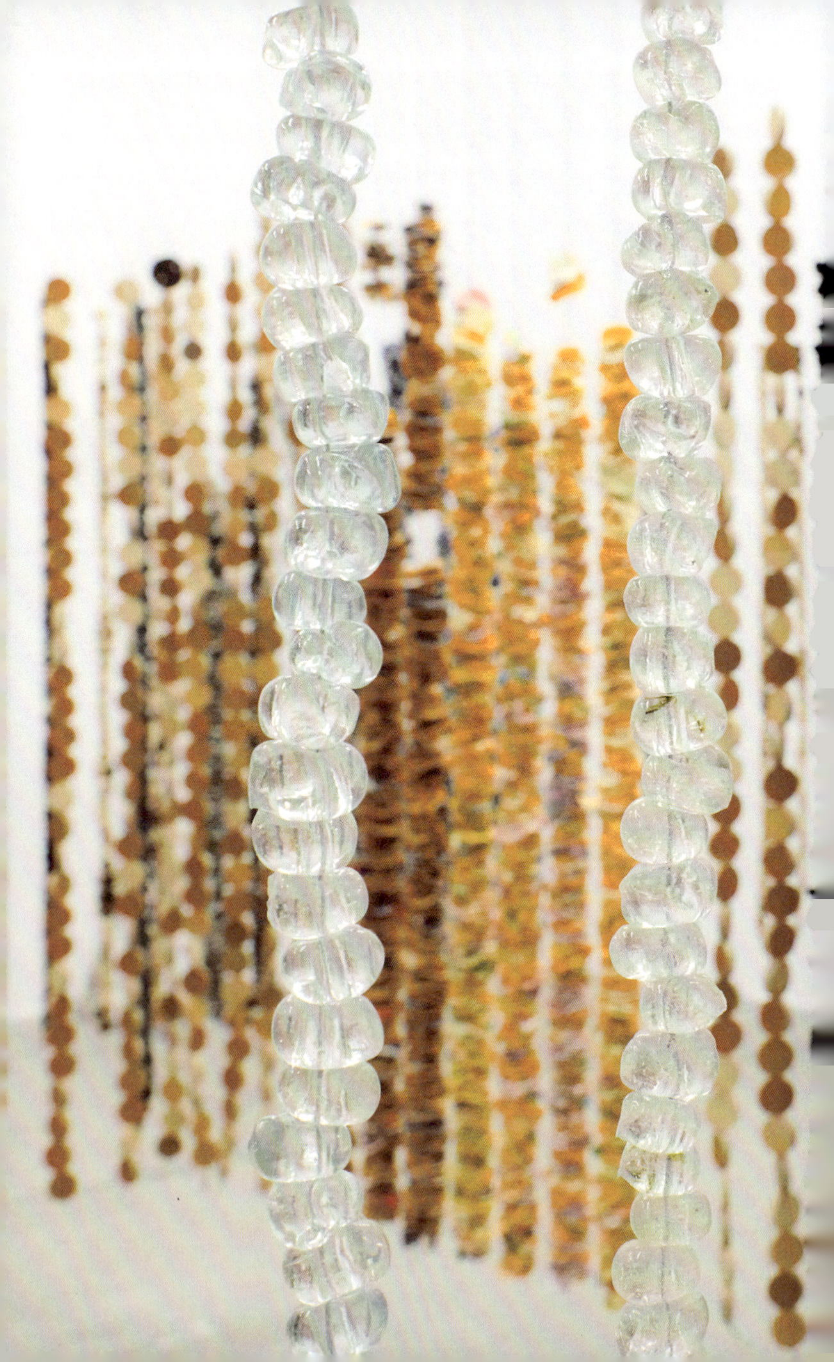

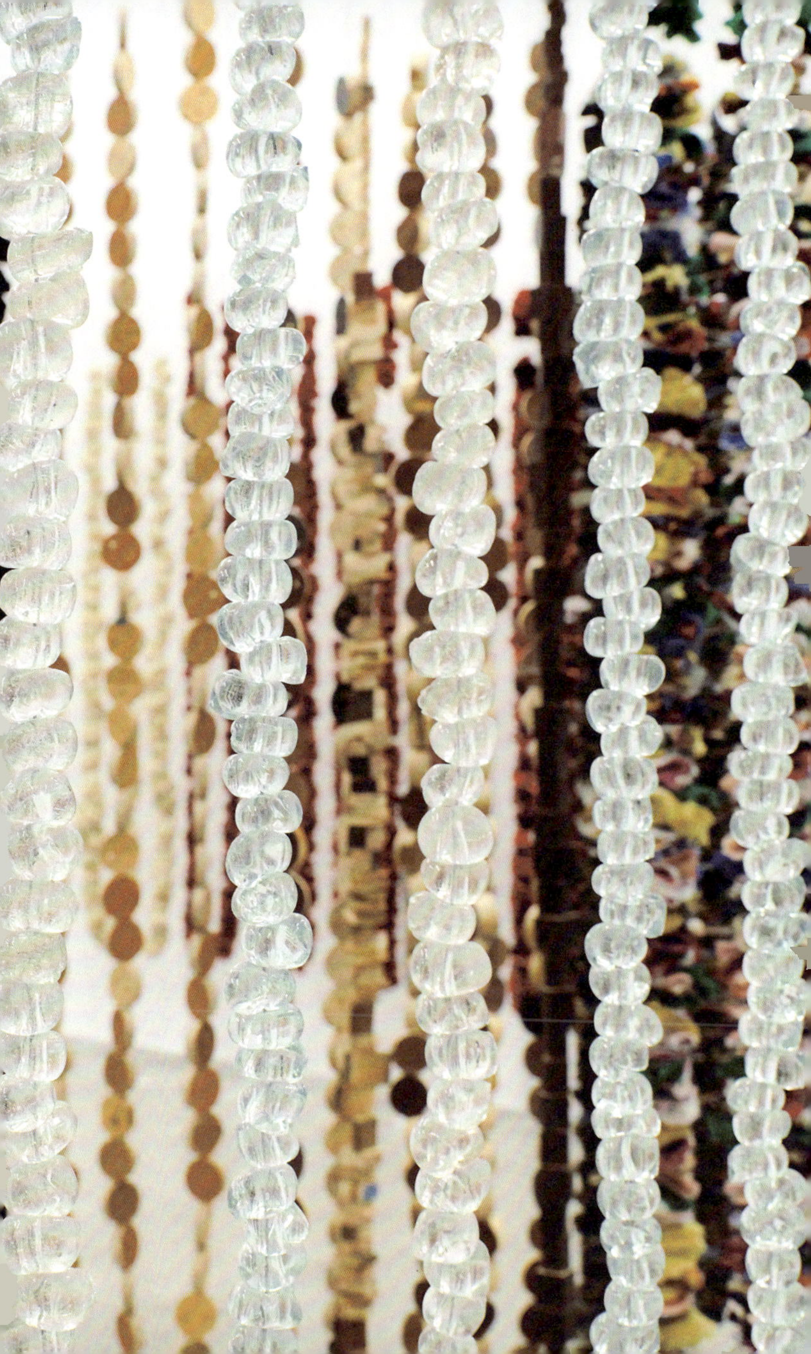

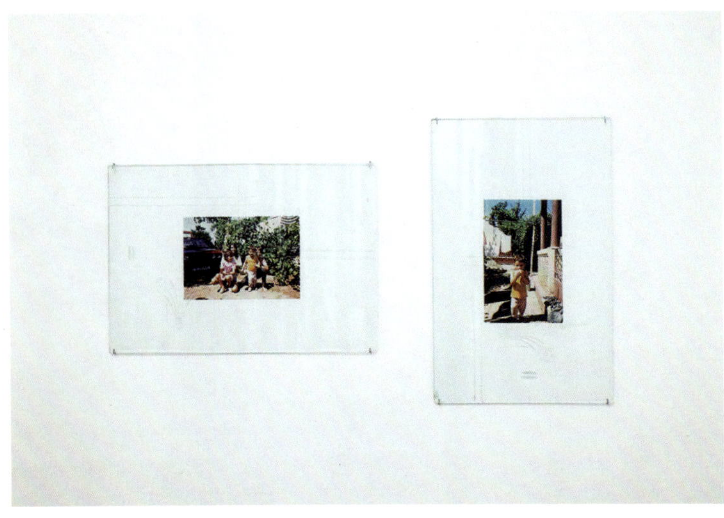

Documentary images from the artist's personal archive, 1996

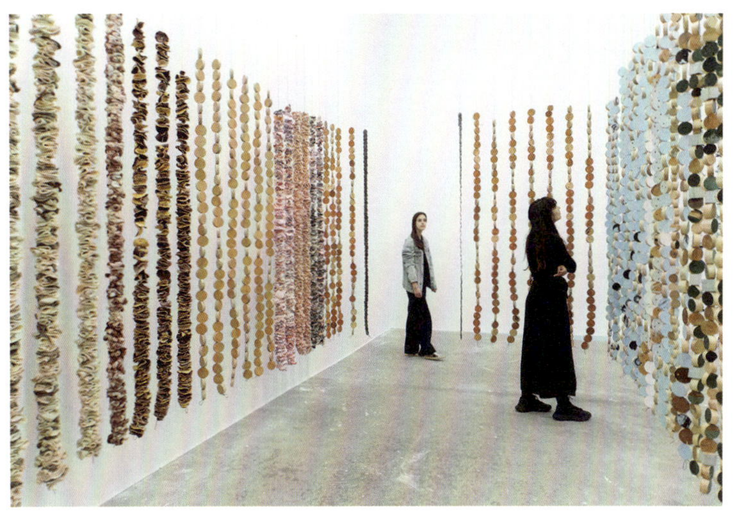

Harvest Time
installation view

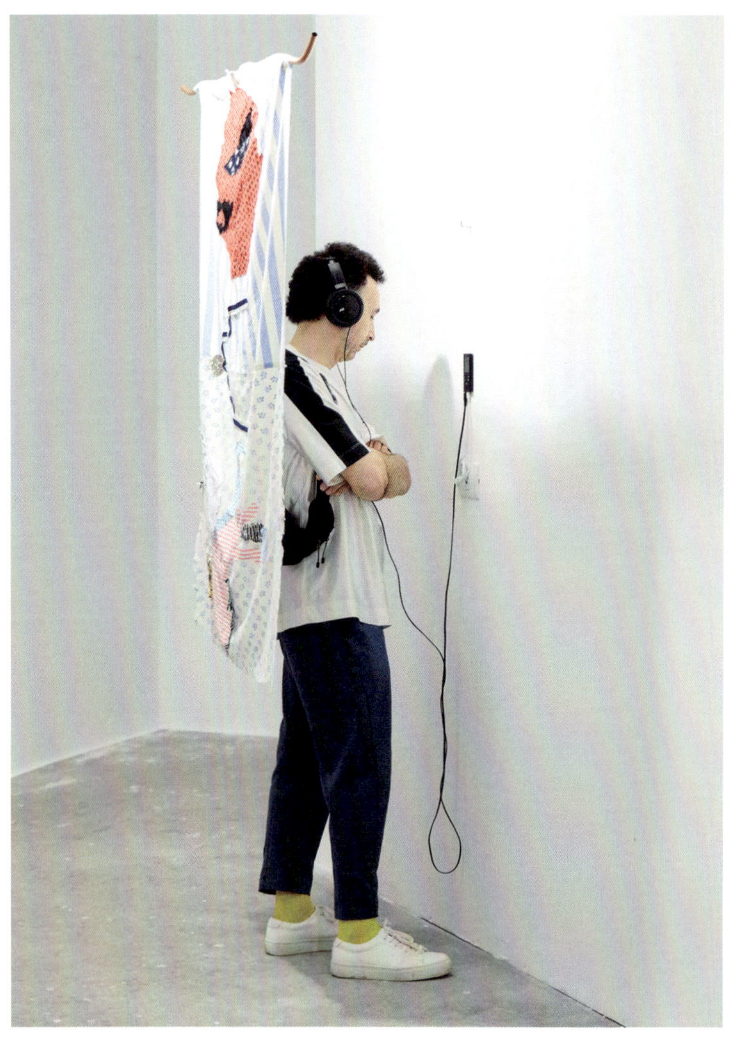

Irina Bujor, *SHIELD no.6
(FROM BRUISES...TO GOOD WILL)*, 2022
sound installation (various textiles, soft copper tube,
headphones, anti-homophobia sports medal by MozaiQ),
54sec

*TRIUMF AMIRIA LOVE LETTER TO
IRINA BUJOR
TRIUMF AMIRIA LOVE LETTER TO
MIHAI MIHALCEA*

10. 06 – 23. 07. 2022
curator: Kilobase Bucharest

Continuing the curatorial format "LOVE LETTER TO
[...]", created in 2021 as part of the TRIUMF AMIRIA
concept, KILOBASE BUCHAREST and KUNSTHALLE
BEGA presented TRIUMF AMIRIA LOVE LETTER TO
IRINA BUJOR and TRIUMF AMIRIA LOVE LETTER TO
MIHAI MIHALCEA - two exhibitions which brought
together queer statements, in a dialogue about the
possibility of revisiting and resizing of worlds that,
rather than divergent, overlap and intertwine. Mihai
Mihalcea's exhibition revealed a process, both subtle
and intense, of negotiating with the artistic identities
assumed over time, the "unit view" becoming the
means of developing his artistic practice. In parallel,
Irina Bujor's exhibition talked about a tireless attempt
to redefine her universe, in which empathy, identity,
and the future were infused with always unexpected
meanings.

TRIUMF AMIRIA LOVE LETTER TO IRINA BUJOR
exhibition view

next spread / cover image

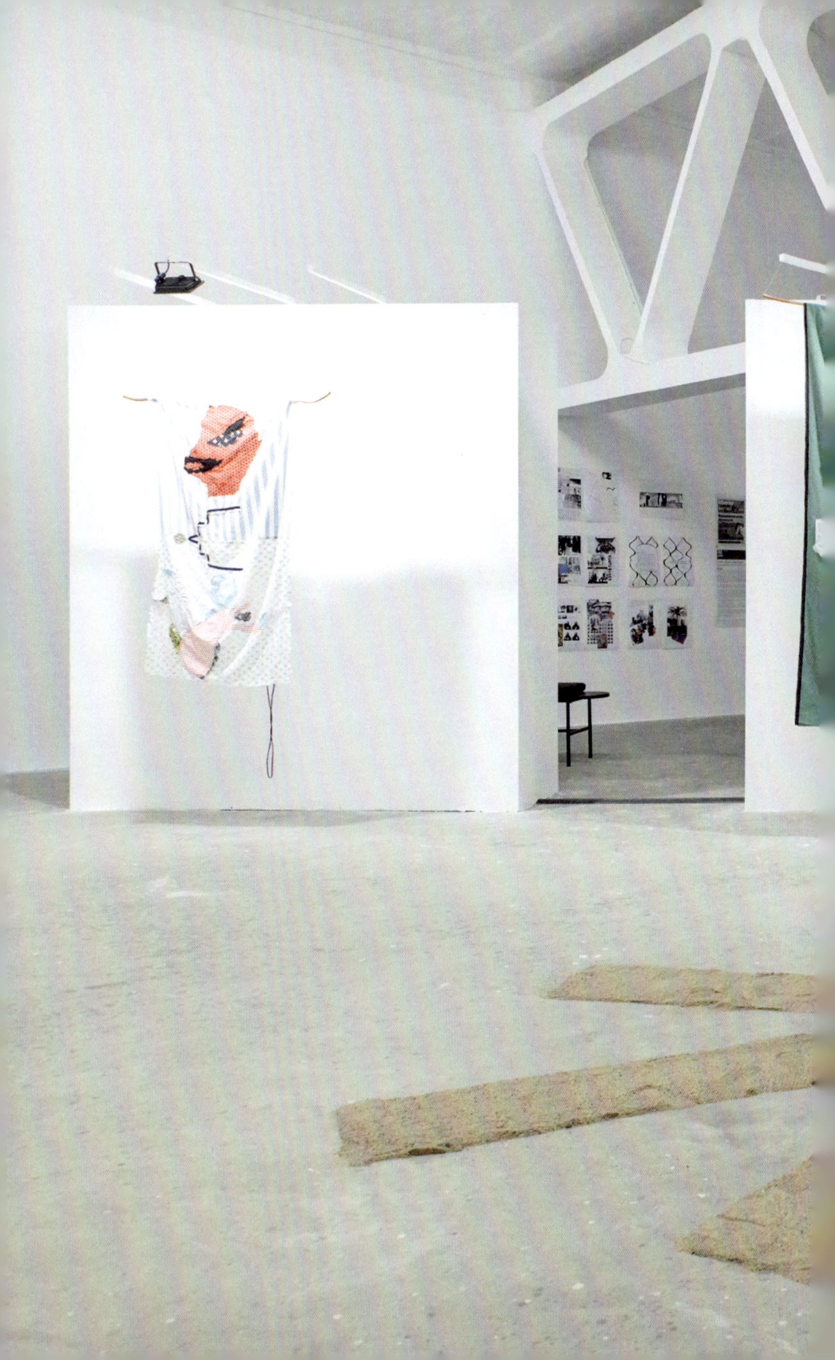

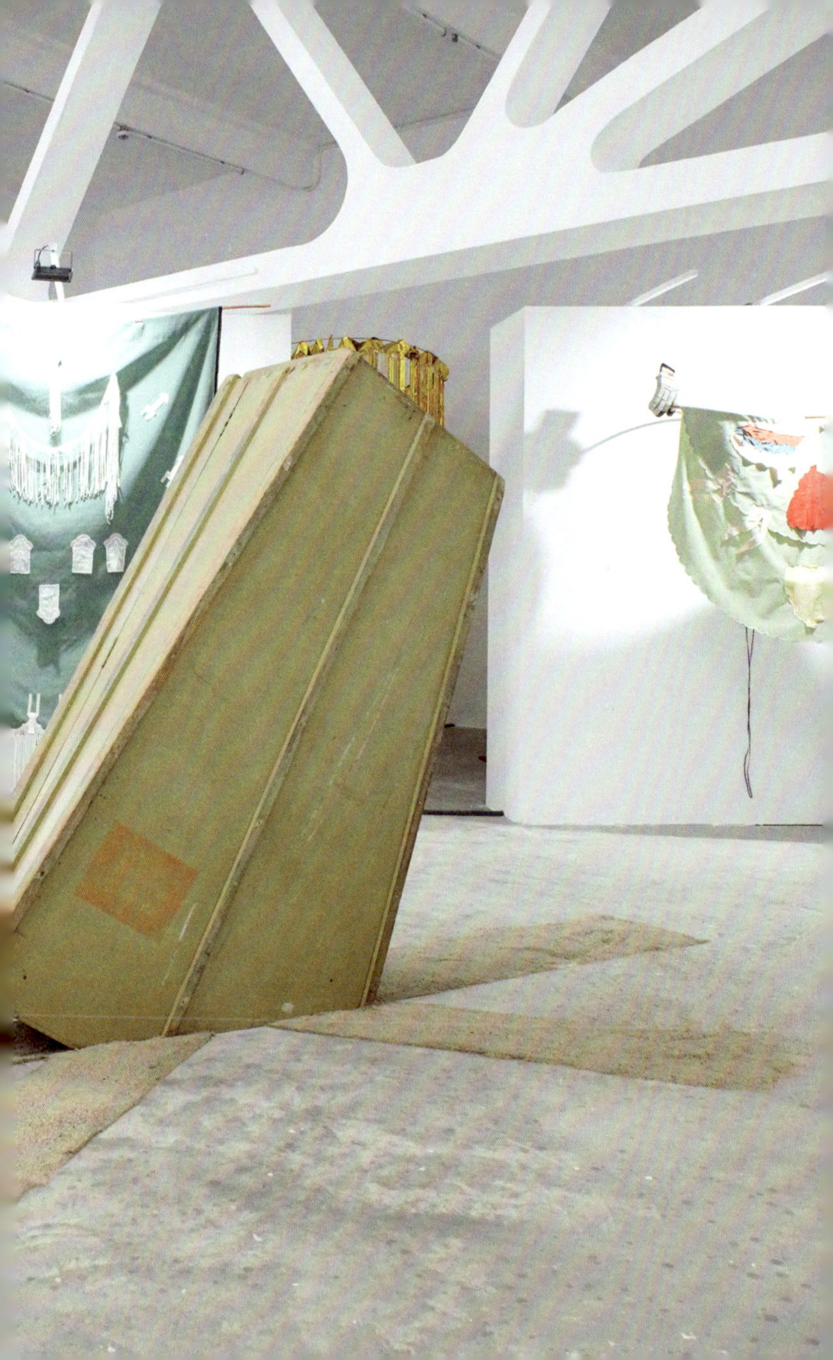

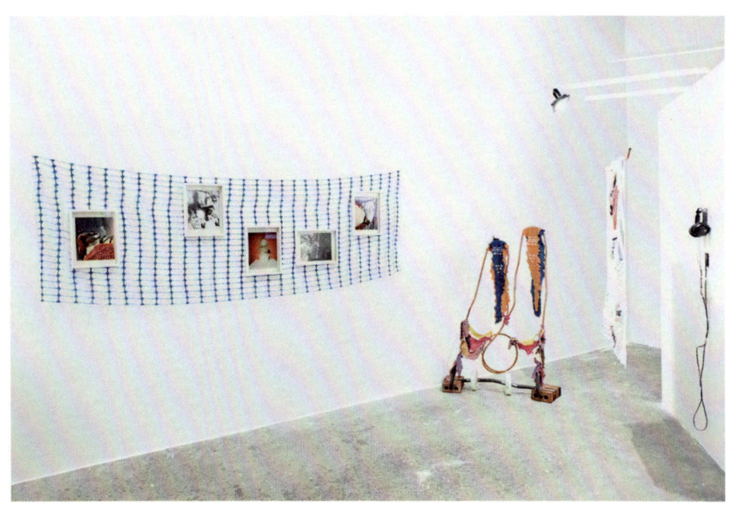

TRIUMF AMIRIA LOVE LETTER TO IRINA BUJOR
exhibition view

Irina Bujor develops her practices mainly in relation
to the particular context offered by small towns in
Romania and Germany. Her artworks are based on
formal associations that open a singular poetic vein;
multi-layered images and installations highlight the
fragility and instability that question our seemingly
secure reality. Applying a wide variety of artistic
strategies, Irina develops a multifaceted practice
around common phenomena that go unnoticed in the
topics she addresses - laughter, gender, factories that
produce popular culture and things that saturate other
things - and tools that constantly recalibrate
her universe.

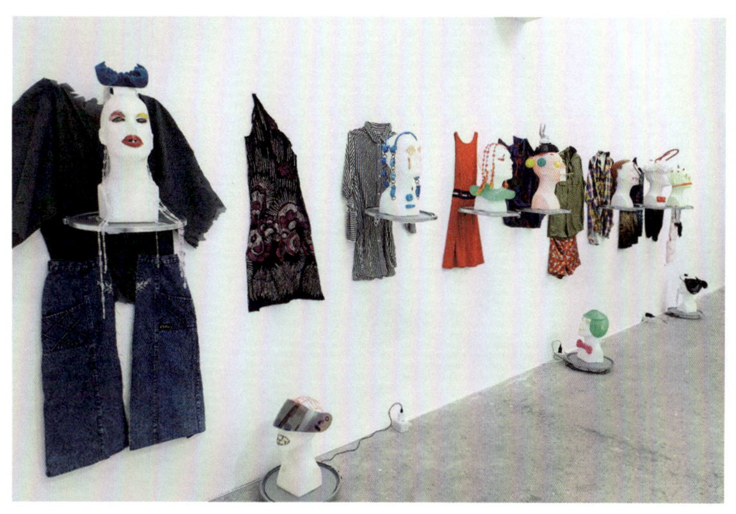

Irina Bujor, *TV On Acid [series]*, 2019 – 2021
installation with 10 characters: Je suis La Regina,
Jon Alimentar, Digital Dan, TubyRub Preciosa,
Fane the Kid, ExpertOfAll Nelu, Charmer Costel,
Diamond Diamond Damian, Seksi Adriana de
România, ISGODB (IStrikeGoldOnDailyBasis) textiles,
mannequins, accessories, metal caps, rotating stands

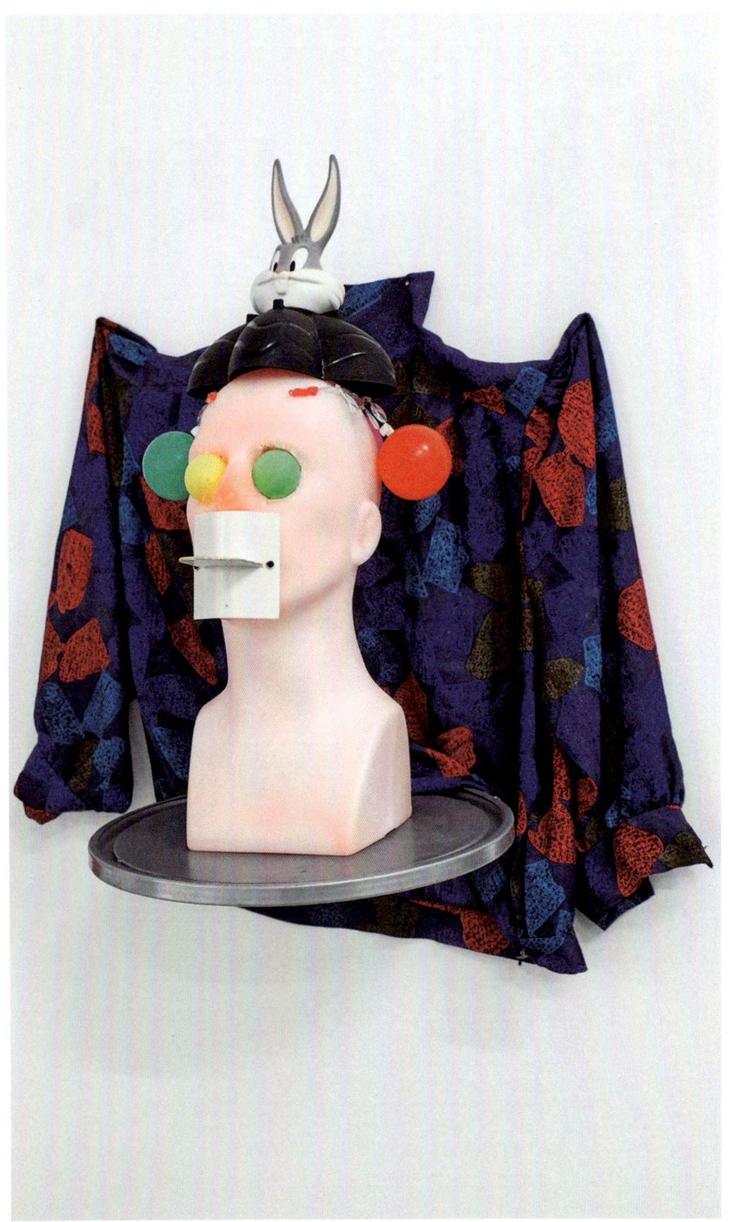

Irina Bujor, *TV On Acid [series]*, 2019 – 2021
installation with 10 characters: Je suis La Regina,
Jon Alimentar, Digital Dan, TubyRub Preciosa,
Fane the Kid, ExpertOfAll Nelu, Charmer Costel,
Diamond Diamond Damian, Seksi Adriana de
România, ISGODB (IStrikeGoldOnDailyBasis) textiles,
mannequins, accessories, metal caps, rotating stands
(detail)

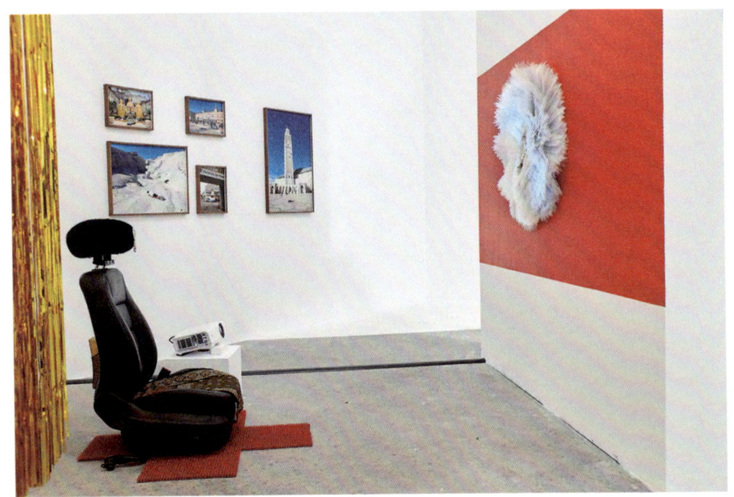

TRIUMF AMIRIA LOVE LETTER TO MIHAI MIHALCEA
exhibition view

Mihai Mihalcea is an artist and choreographer based in Bucharest. He created and co-founded fundamental structures and projects that led to the international recognition of Romanian contemporary dance creation. Between 1994 – 2009 he presented his choreographic works in institutions around the world, and in 2010 he assumed a fictitious artistic identity, Farid Fairuz, under which he continued his activity until 2019, making choreographic works and performances, live and for the camera, presented both in the context of visual arts and contemporary dance. Mihai continues his activity at the intersection between visual arts and dance, keeping a fresh eye on his artistic development.

Kilobase Bucharest

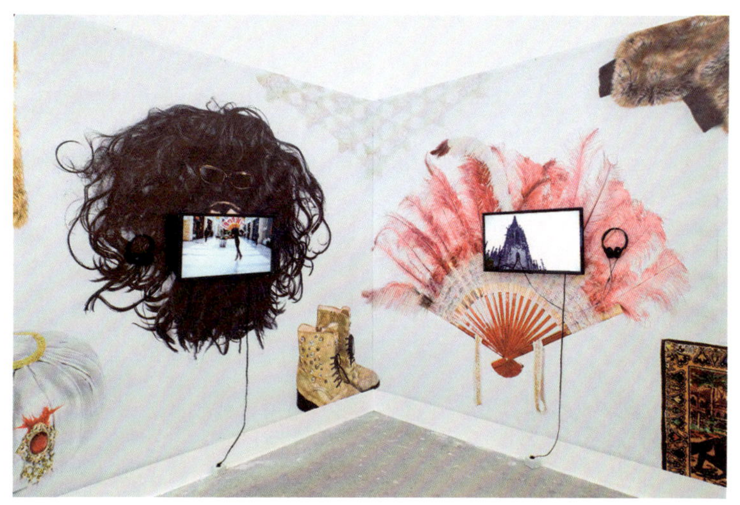

Mihai Mihalcea, *Documenting Farid Fairuz*, 2010 – 2019, installation (2021): reproductions from the Farid Fairuz documentary archive (props, press articles) & "Afifarid II" (6min 48sec) and "Lament (not Mecca, not Rome)" (10min 42sec) video performances (detail)

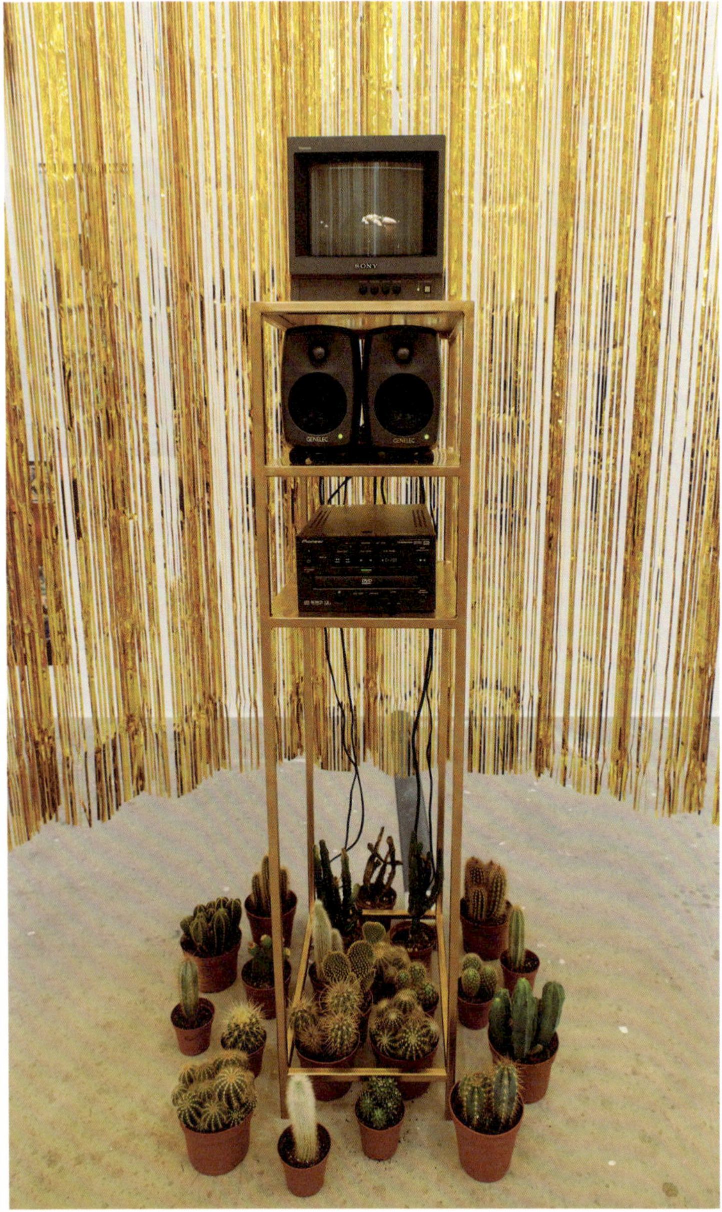

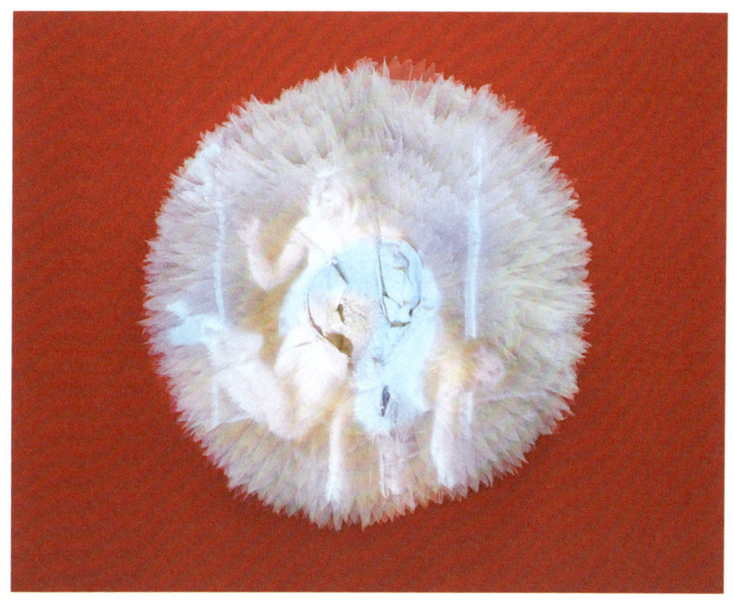

Mihai Mihalcea, *Act IV (A Disobedient Sequence Sliding Out Of Context)*, installation, 2021: car seat, tutu dress, fotă (traditional romanian skirt), kavuk (ottoman turban), book, pvc floor mat, video 5min 07sec
(detail)

Mihai Mihalcea, *Memory for Sale*, 2022
installation, 2022: edited video documentation,
21min 01sec (recorded at Podewil, Berlin, 2002), metal shelving, fringe tinsel curtain, cacti
choreography and interpretation: Mihai Mihalcea
musical collage from: Premdas Hegoda, Jerome Soudain
(detail)

previous page

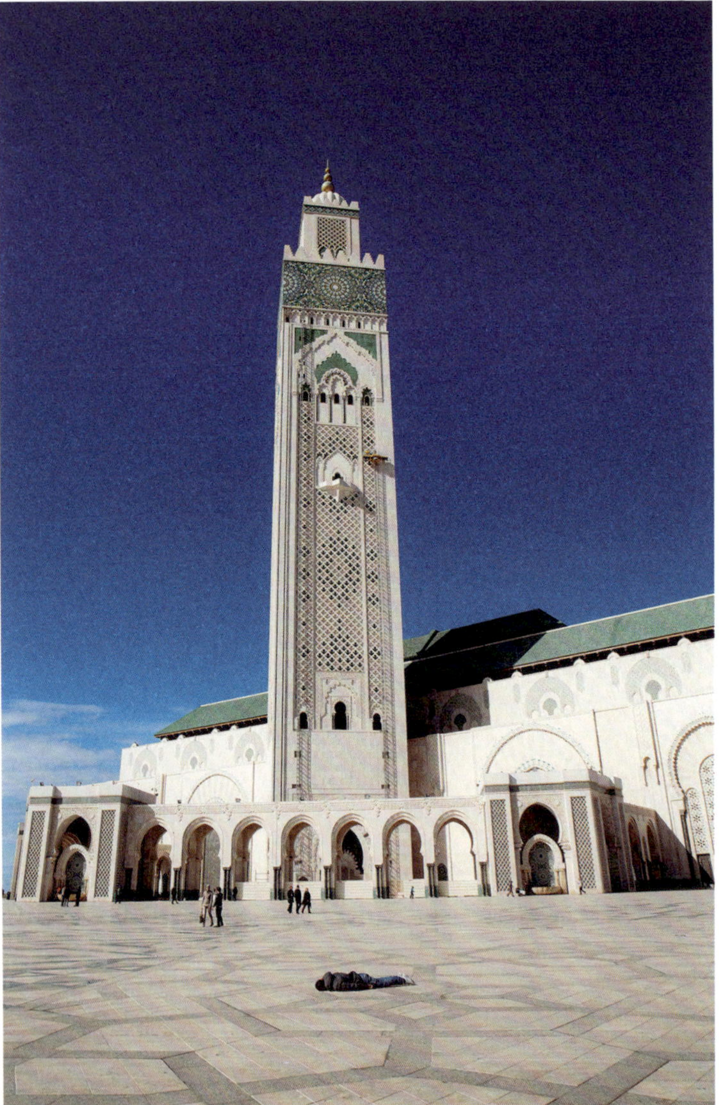

Mihai Mihalcea, *Leap into the work (Casablanca)*, 2015
series (2004 – ongoing)
performance for camera;
colour photographs, digital print

previous page

TRIUMF AMIRIA LOVE LETTER TO MIHAI MIHALCEA
exhibition view

next spread

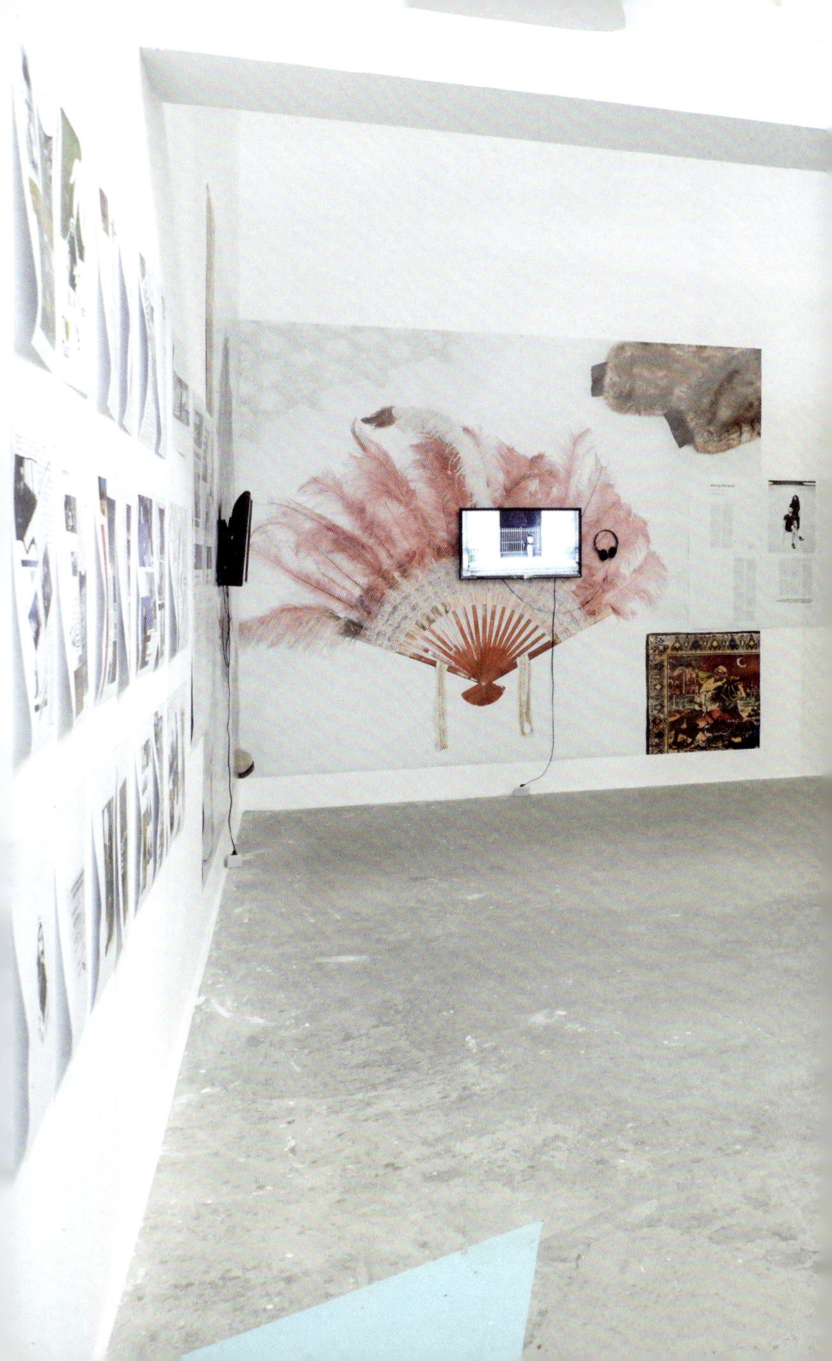

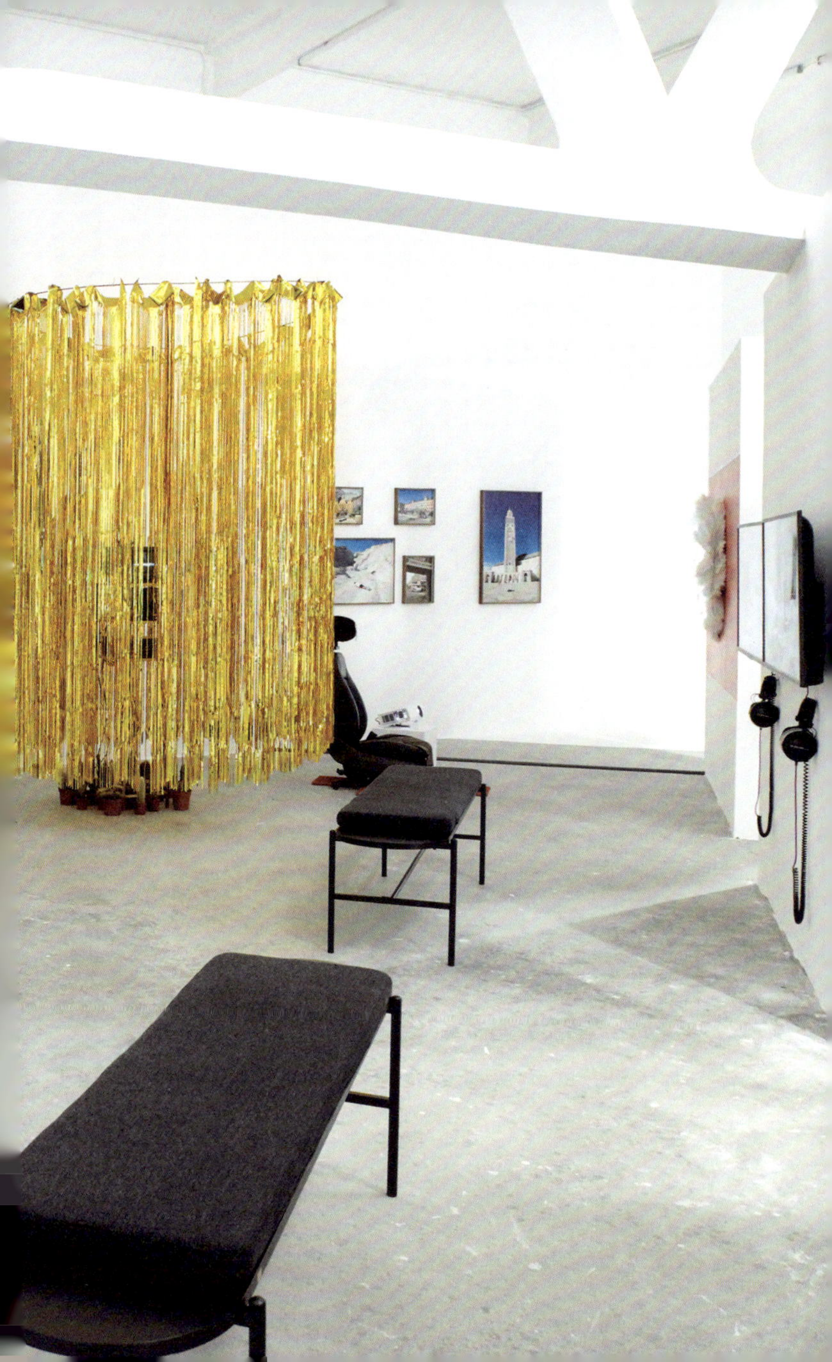

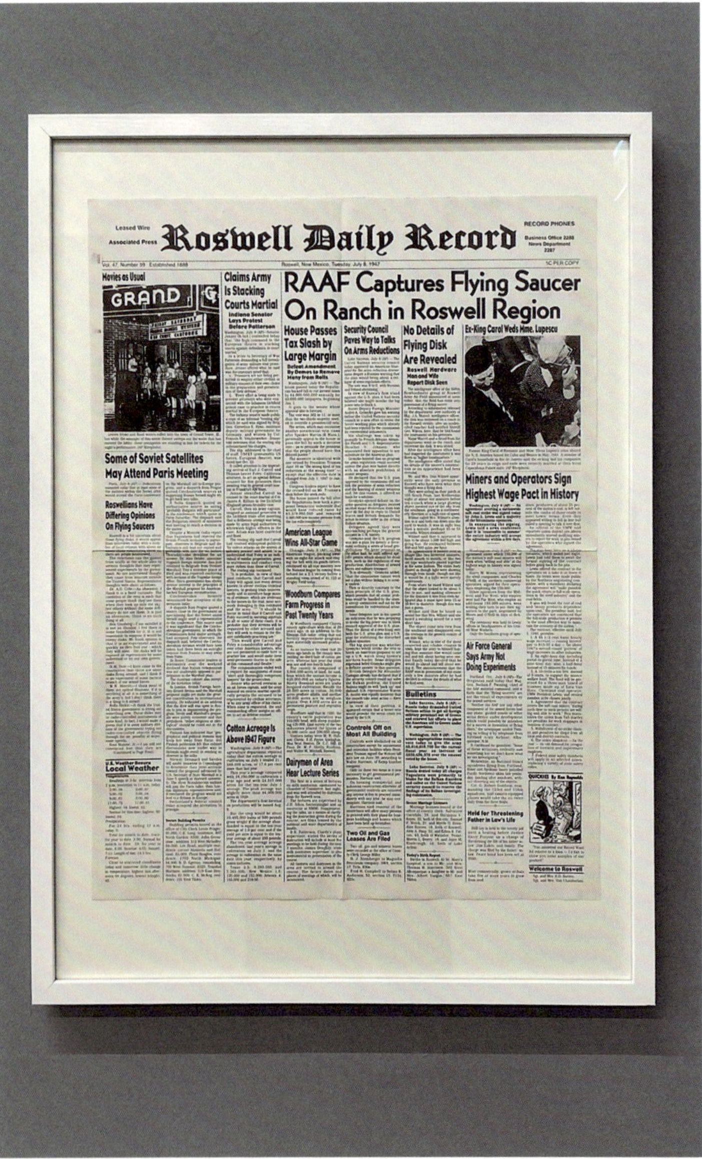

Front page of the *Roswell Daily Record*, July 8, 1947

The Approximate Man 3.0
Mihai Zgondoiu

08. 04 – 22. 05. 2022

2022: Spatial Odyssey
(The Return of the Approximate Man)

The Approximate Man 3.0, an exhibition of Mihai Zgondoiu, conceived for the space of Kunsthalle Bega Box, has the value of a manifesto (even if not suggested clearly). Meaning it has a programmatic and visionary dimension, comments about both current conversions and an uncertain future, proposes excellent and compelling images, and possesses provocative rhetorics while infused with irony, a sign of particular critical spirit knowledge. The theme, or what shall we call it? The purpose? Space. More precisely, outer space with all its realms of extraterrestrial beings and the various intellectual ways of exploring them. To reveal, interrogate and comment not only on approximate individuals (with all the potential meanings) but also on possible worlds those half-real, half-imaginary universes inhabited, how else than by the approximate people?

The generic syntagm undoubtedly refers to the indisputable Tristan Tzara, more precisely to his volume, *L'homme approximatif*, published in 1931. In addition, the exhibition's title suggests the ambiguity of the characters connected to these unearthly universes, which we have already mentioned, that Mihai Zgondoiu researches and works with, that is, the ALIENated man, the alien endowed with an approximate human identity. These references also indicate two of the leading resources defining the art of Mihai Zgondoiu: the historical avant-garde and the paranormal subculture.

Within the exhibition, the avant-garde heritage encounters the traditional "studies" in mysteries and paranormal, parallel and extraterrestrial worlds, with a sarcastically viewed personal mythology, which becomes the conceptual axis and the "resource" of this exhibition. The artist's interest in this area is long-standing, and his research is comprehensive. The outcome? Sketches, archived documents, and produced, cut and altered images.

The exhibition is designed as an installation (placement that speaks for Zgondoiu's curatorial aptitudes), an otherworldly environment conquered by the large-scale personal drawings, transferred from the sketchbook to dark grey walls, white cartography of a non-existing (at least at the moment) world. Among other, more or less obvious, icons and symbols we find here (and everywhere in the exhibition) that alien mask with huge eyes and elongated face, the symbol-image of visitors from other worlds, taken from the arsenal of science fiction. The artist's drawings and collages are also displayed in the video edit on screens placed in a pyramid, an emblem of the creative power (of the sun) and immortality, most probably, of the Approximate Man of Zgondoiu.

Since we mentioned otherworldly characters, we should say that the artist presents a gallery of oval-shaped portraits on ceramic plates, similar to

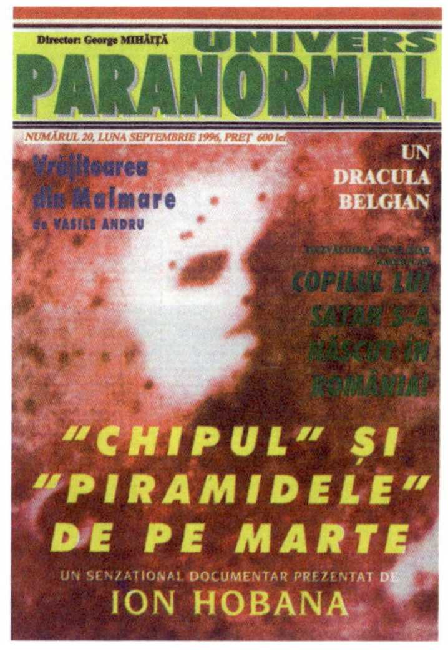

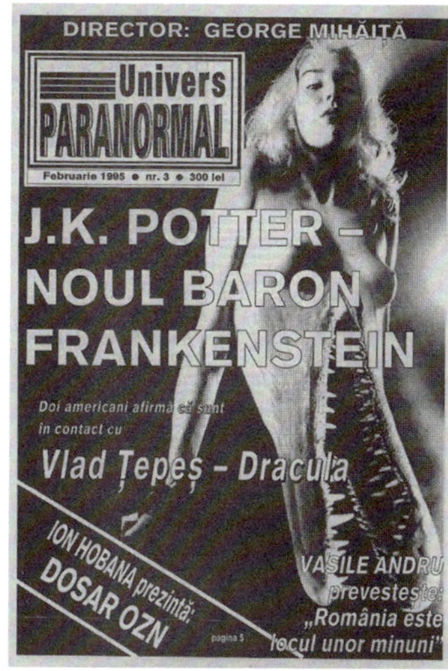

Covers of *Univers Paranormal* magazine,
no. 20, September 1996
no. 3, February 1995

those on funerary stones, this time dedicated to aliens destroyed in films. An equal mix of humor and appreciation. Moreover, in an ironic twist, the artist presents the framed first page of the American newspaper, *Roswell Daily Record,* issued on July 8, 1947, announcing the capture of a flying saucer next to the announcement of the marriage of King Carol II of Romania in exile. The correlation has powerful meanings, revealing coincidences regarding alienation and floating destiny in the eye of the artist.

The leading role in this approximate world is taken by the bibliography (pop magazines and obscure

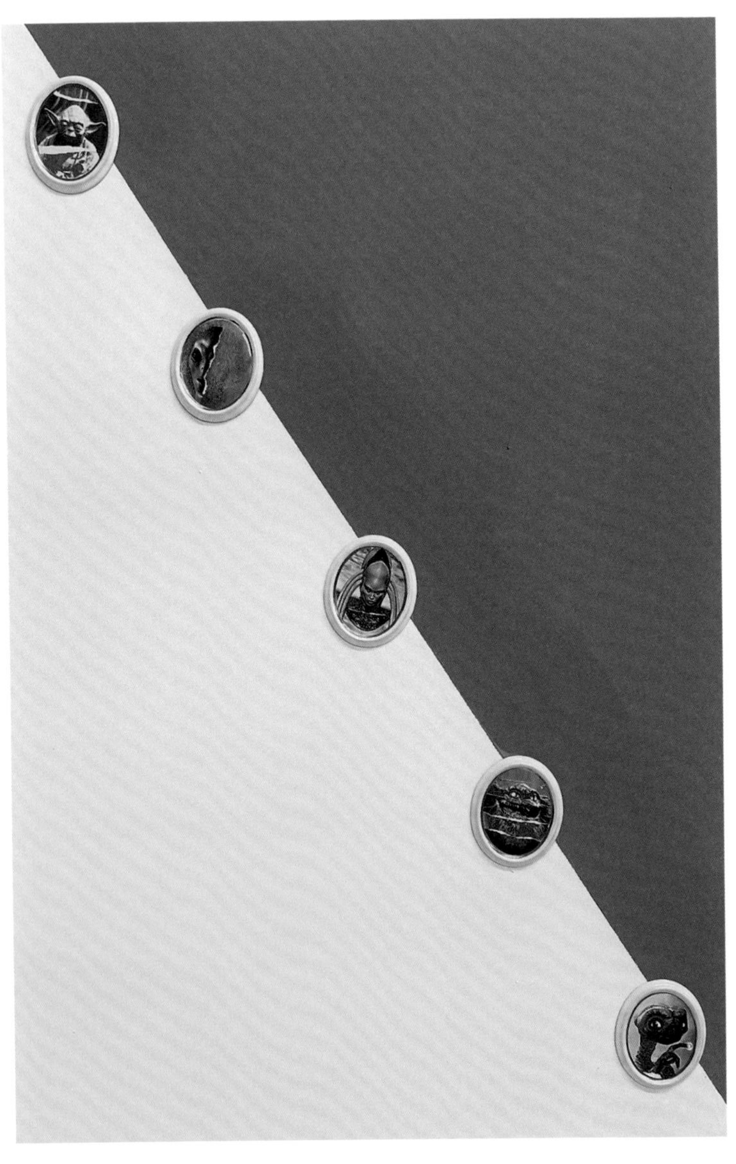

EXTRAfaces – 12 Typologies of Aliens, 2016
print, collage on Bohemian ceramics

publications) dedicated to UFOs, paranormal
activities, circumstantial universes, magical beings, and
quasi-religious miracles. Most of these are gathered
in consistent "codices," true bibles of ufology and
the paranormal, solemnly placed on lecterns that
equally resemble church furniture and the devices of
a SF spaceship, a suggestion amplified by the esoteric
purple light flooding the place. The stellar sound
environment, etherical, aerated, and mysterious in
turn surrounds the people and the works.

The numerical mention in the title of the exhibition
refers to the current technological lexis, naming
the next generation of the internet: the metaverse,
decentralised usage, the art of artificial intelligence
(AI), NFTs, and clouds. Thus, *The Approximate Man 3.0*
exhibition is, in equal measure, about the actuality
of the Avant-garde and its perpetual return, and
about other worlds, about us, about clouds and the
approximative beings who inhabit them.

Horea Avram

The Approximate Man 3.0
exhibition view
next spread

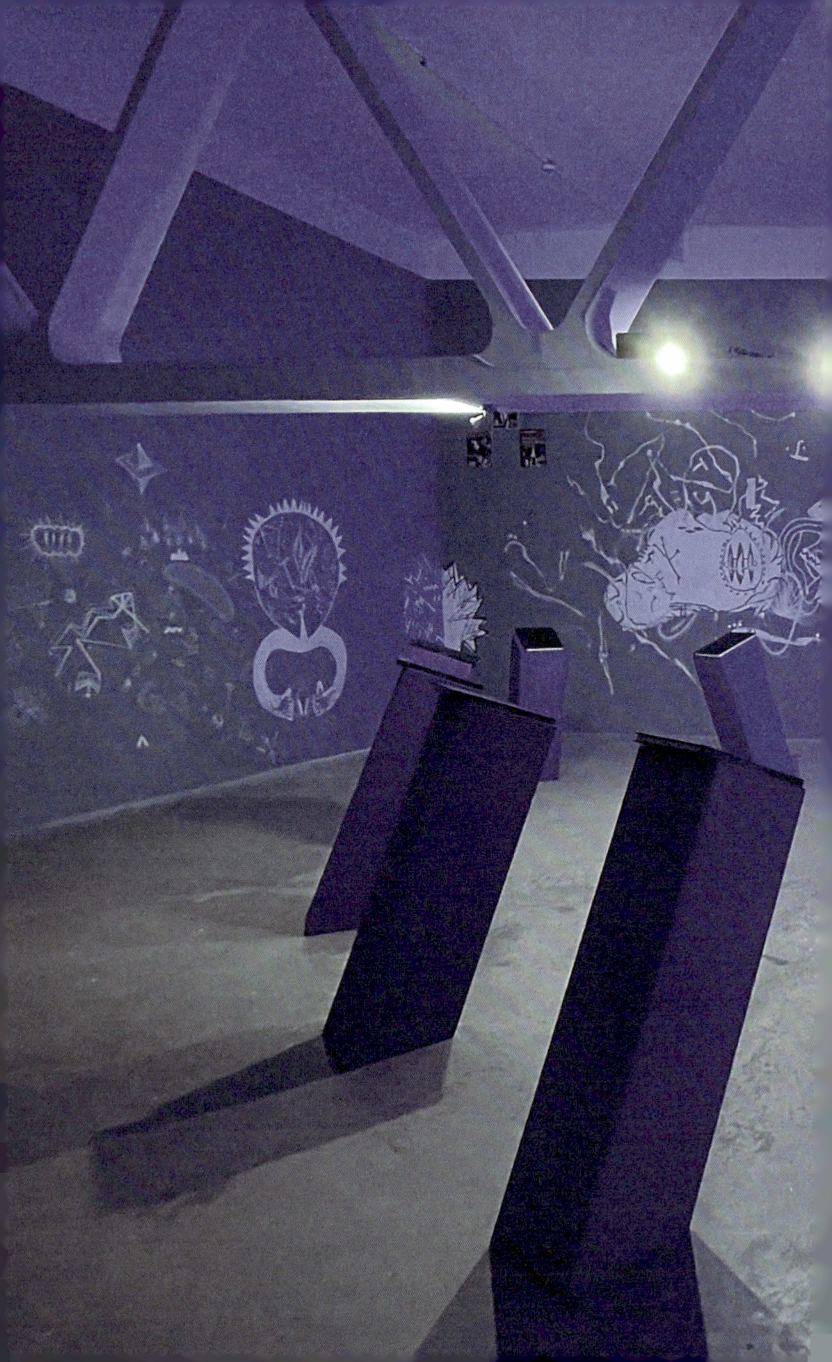

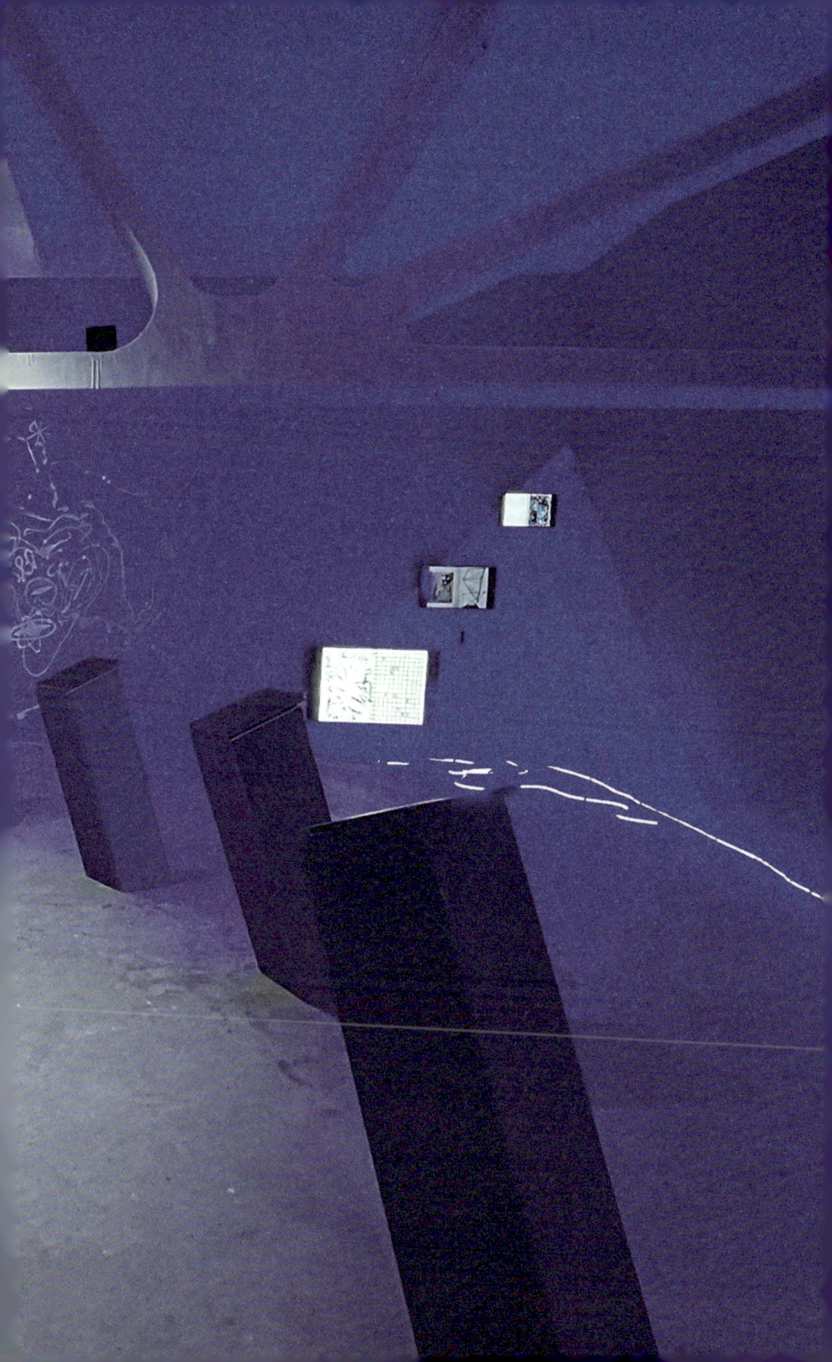

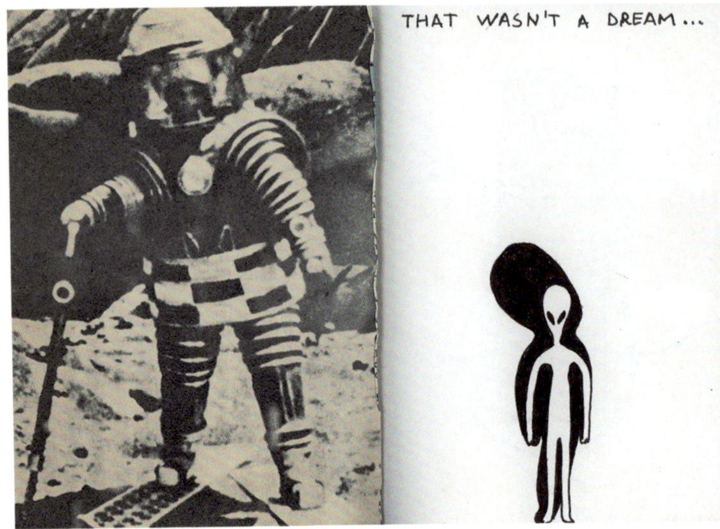

The End of the World notebook, 2012
drawing, collage
(detail)

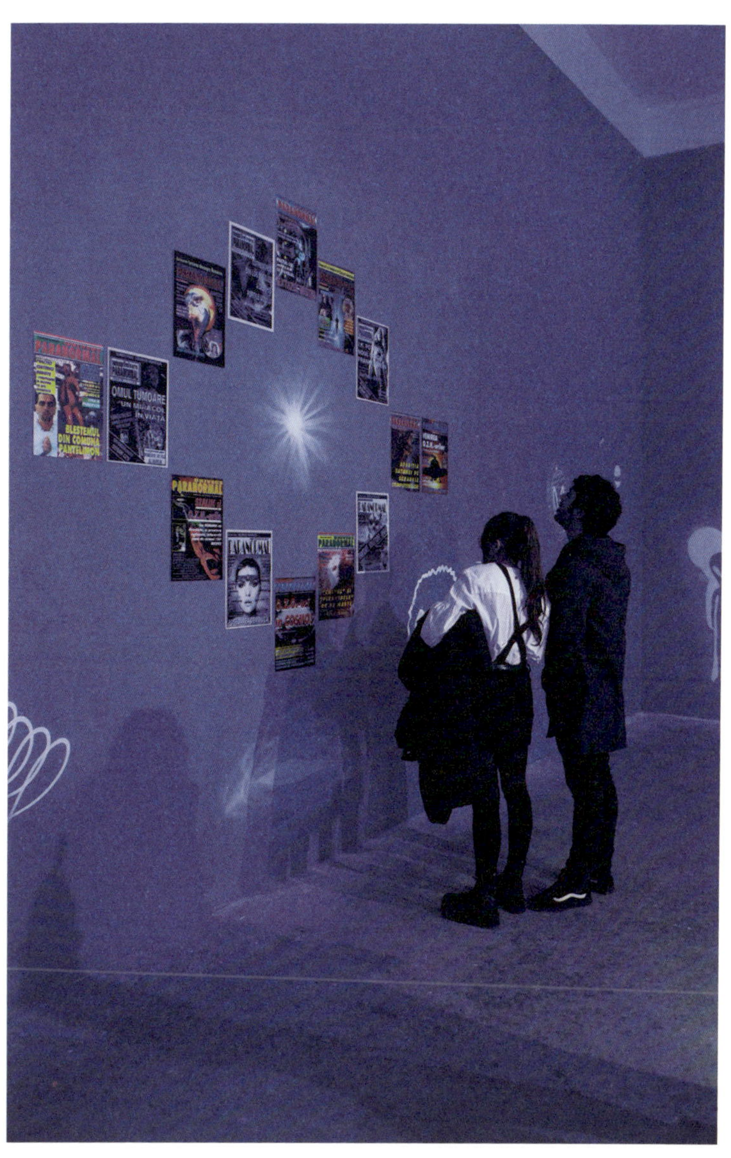

The Approximate Man 3.0
exhibition view

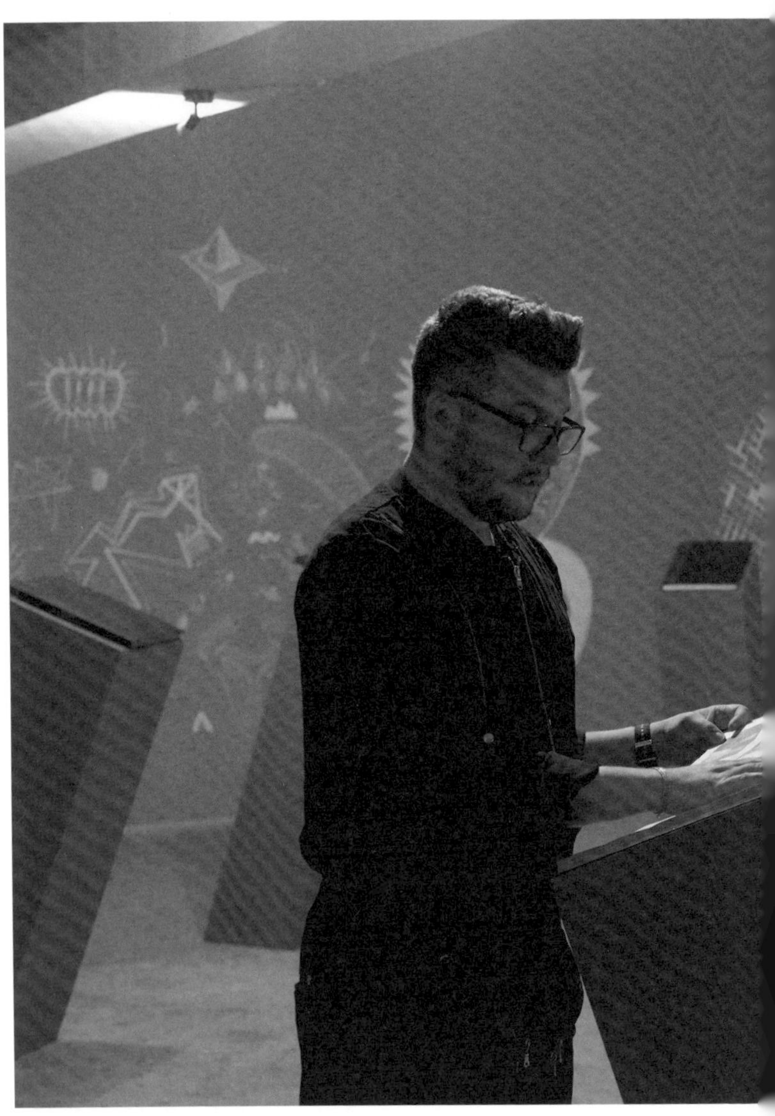

The Approximate Man 3.0
Mihai Zgondoiu performing

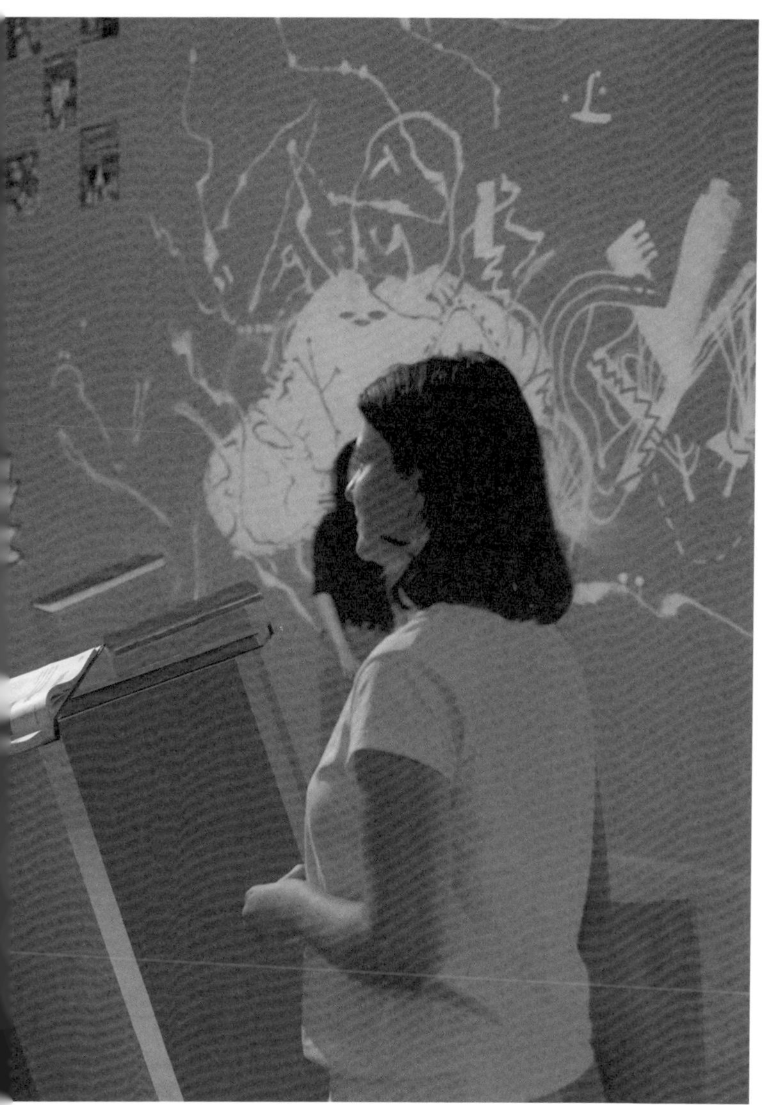

The Approximate Man 3.0
exhibition view

next spread

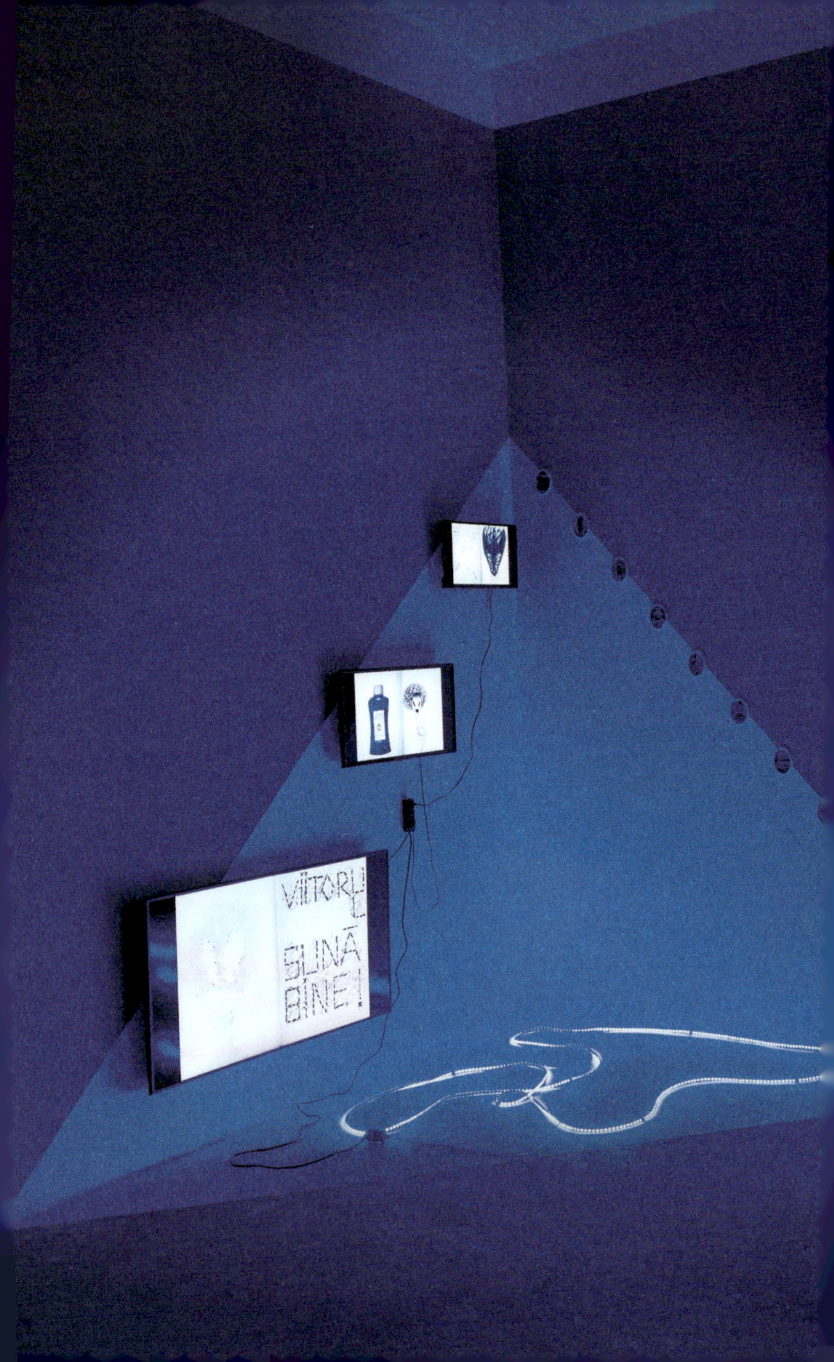

VIITORU
SUNĂ
BINE!

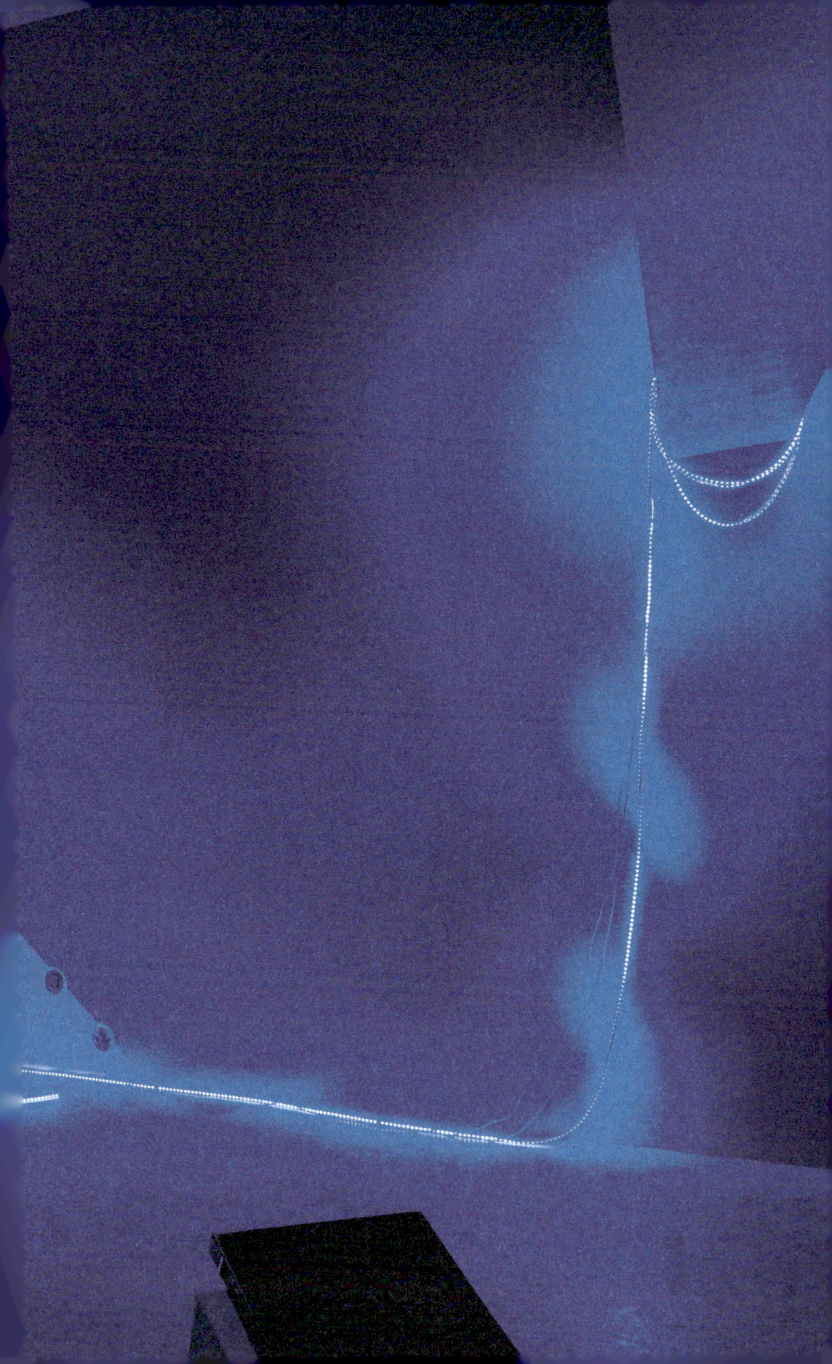

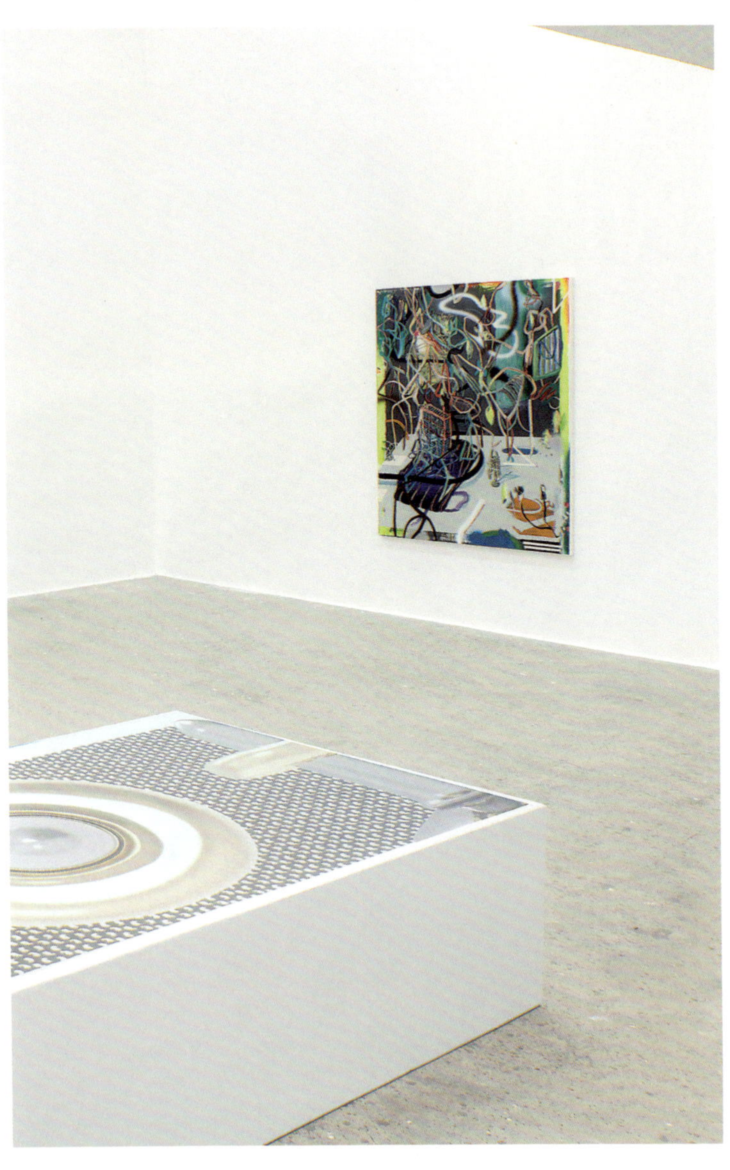

Soft Objects
exhibition view

Soft Objects
Laurian Popa

17. 04 – 15. 05. 2021

Soft objects is a phrase that, at first glance, seems contradictory in the context of this type of visual dialogue, giving the impression that it could even be an oxymoron. The strong and solid objects lose their shape and structure becoming malleable, yielding under the effect of some actions whose sources are unclear. It is not clear what is causing the changes in the properties of these objects, what these deforming forces are, but the visual effect is obvious: the objects are loose, devoid of any structure and deprived of the function which we normally associate them with. Their inner geometry seems to be completely missing being replaced by a new internal organization that reveals the exhaustion of the object as structure, texture and volume. We are talking about another type of image perception whose reference becomes illogical and abstract, but it provides the object with a new anatomy. Using this modest reality of the object (*modest body object*) in the current context, we can make a comparison with a society which becomes dysfunctional in certain circumstances.

We have to deal with an association of functional-dysfunctional images that outlines a fictional world in which the real object is decontextualized and associated with the *arranged* image of the visual compositions that are created. All these *objects* become sources of visual interpretation from which colour and texture are evaded, thus exhausting all the essence of the object which is concentrated into another type of image provided with some substance, in which the reference object is represented pysically, but which transforms into an abstract and non-concrete structure. This creates other landmarks, other directions approached to read the visual image forcing the reception mode.

This topic provides the space, the Kunsthalle Bega Box with a scenic air through which the painting and experimental animation complement each other, offering a narrative thread, and which outlines the installation proposed by me. This dystopia of still nature connects the viewer to another type of visual dialogue, which tries to overcome perceptual blockages, a dialogue that leaves each viewer the chance to form their own idea about the work itself.

Laurian Popa

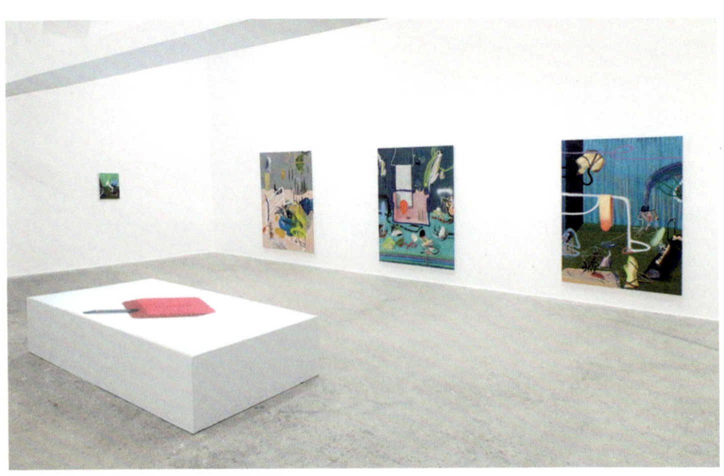

Soft Objects
exhibition view

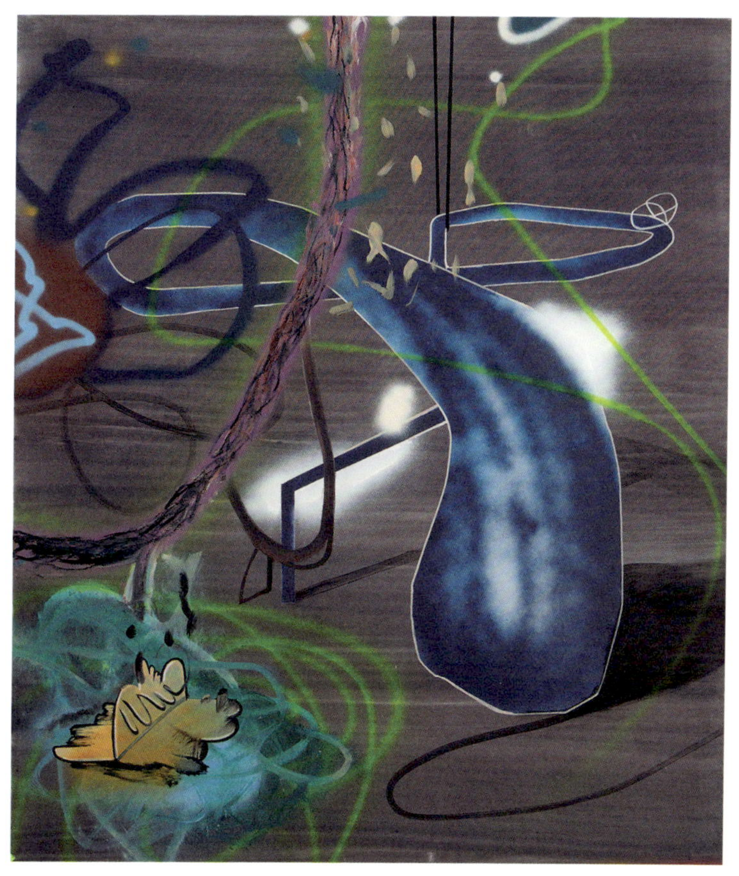

Soft objects, 2021
acrylic and oil on linen, 130x150cm

Still from *Non-Objects*, 2021
3D animation, 4min 16sec

next spread

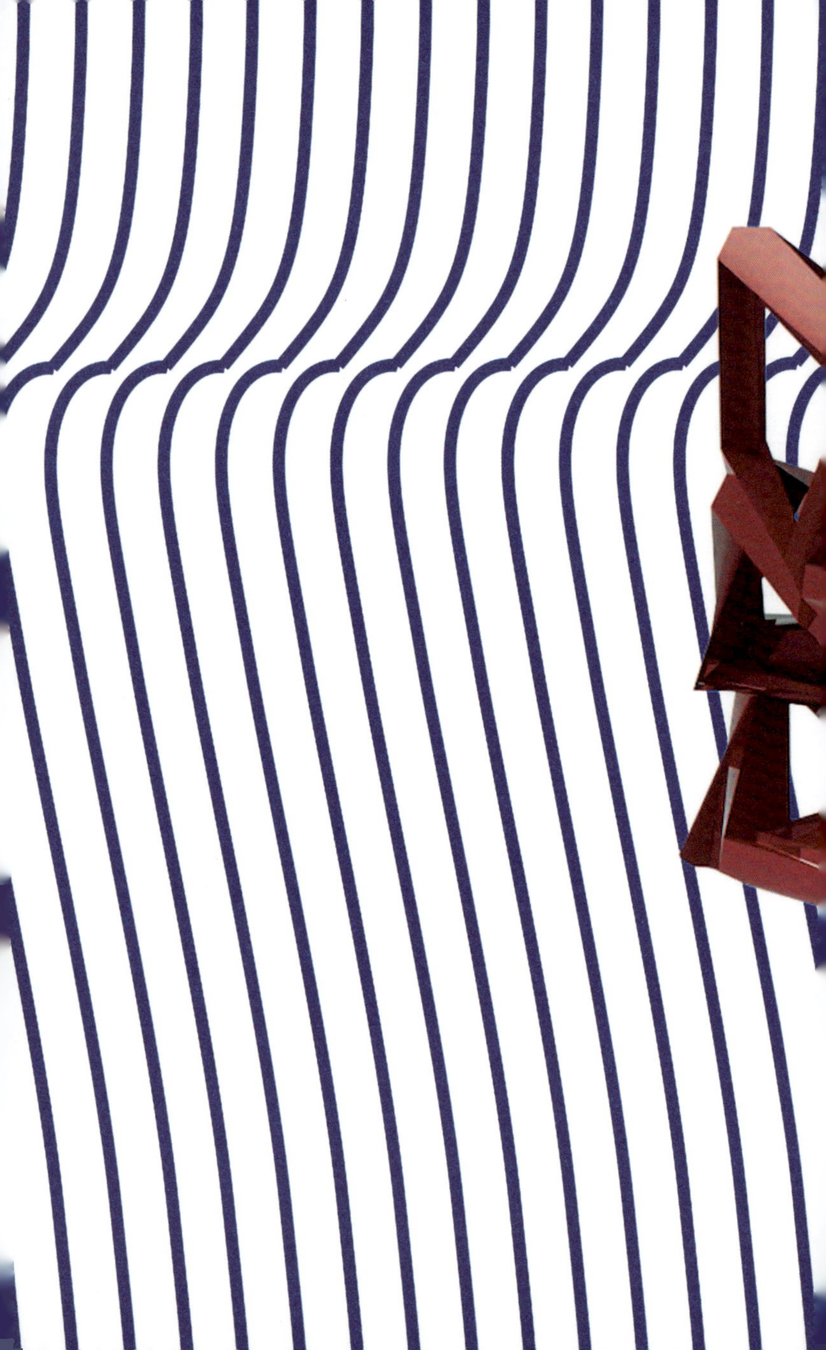

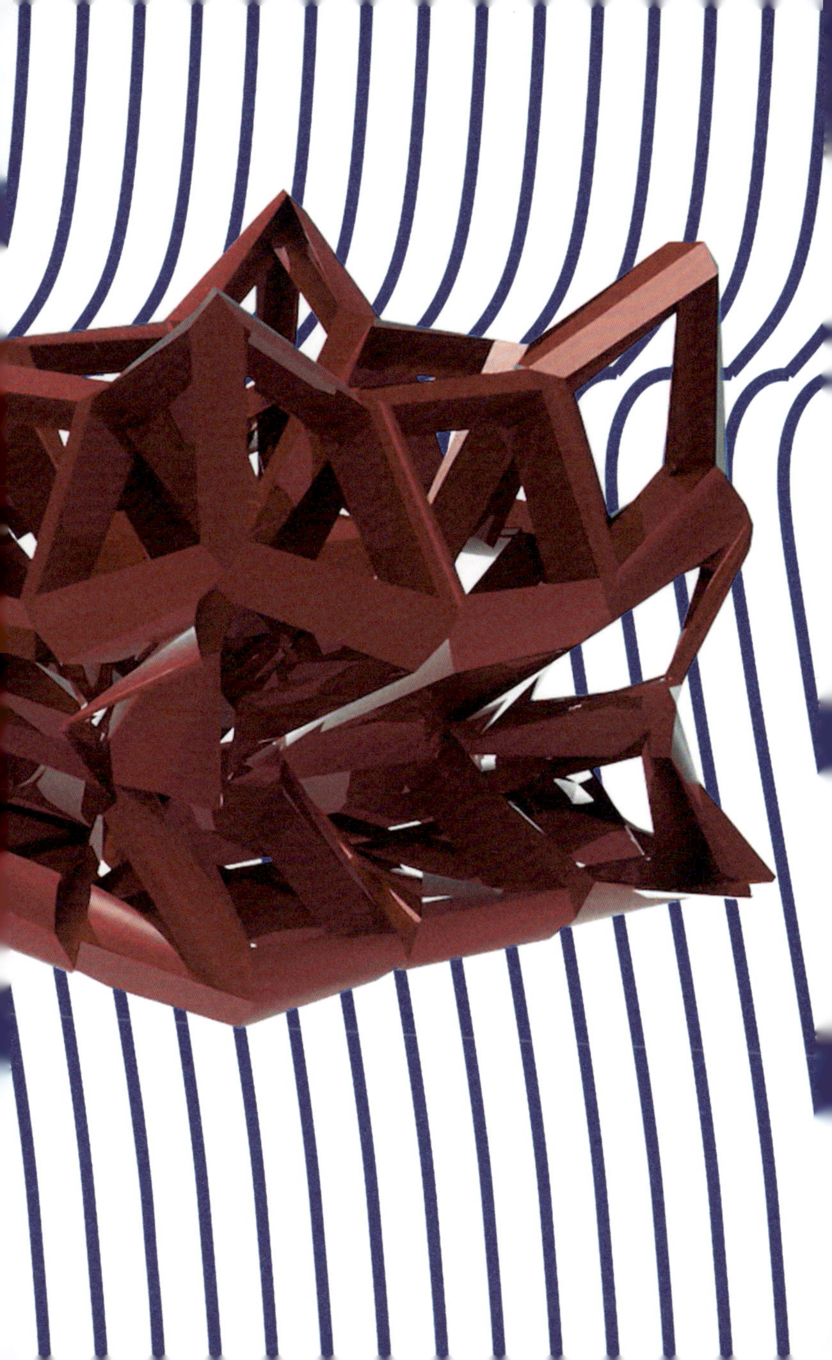

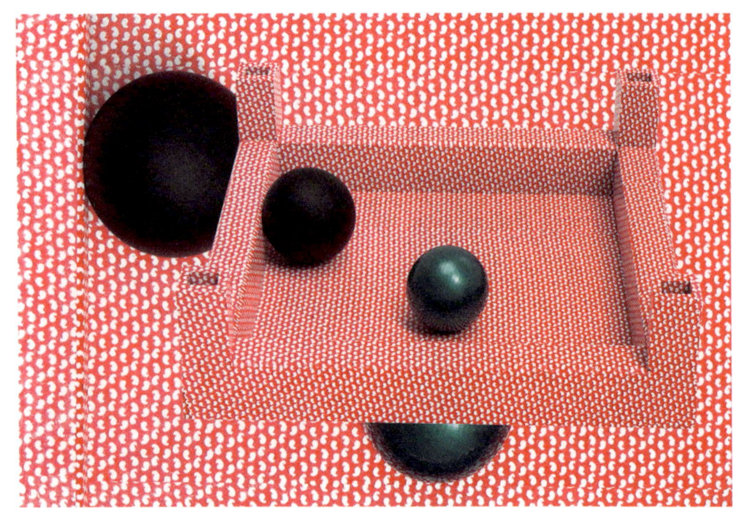

Still from *Non-Objects*, 2021
3D animation, 4min 16sec

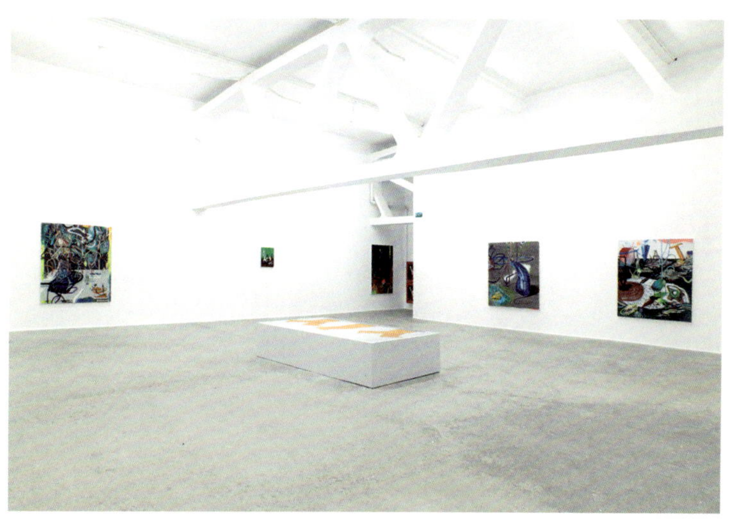

Soft Objects
exhibition view

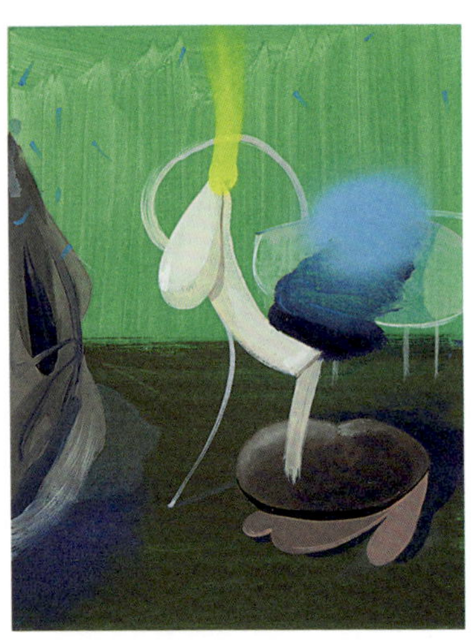

Velvet pillow, 2021
acrylic on linen, 40 x 50 cm

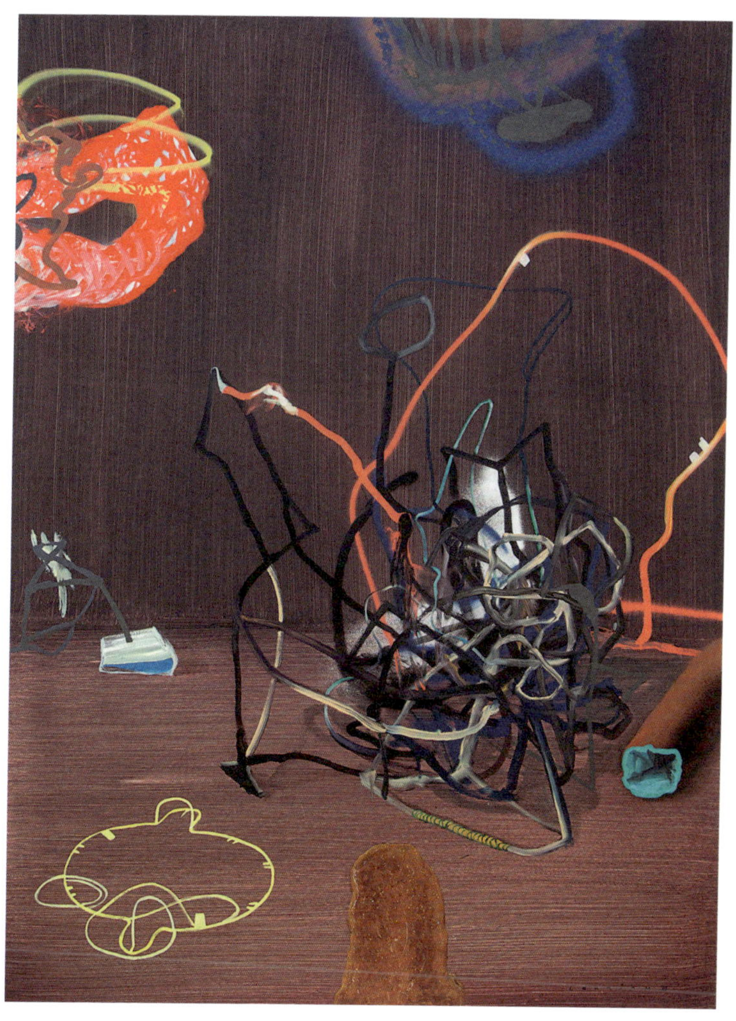

Brown room, 2021
acrylic, oil and latex on linen
150 x 200 cm

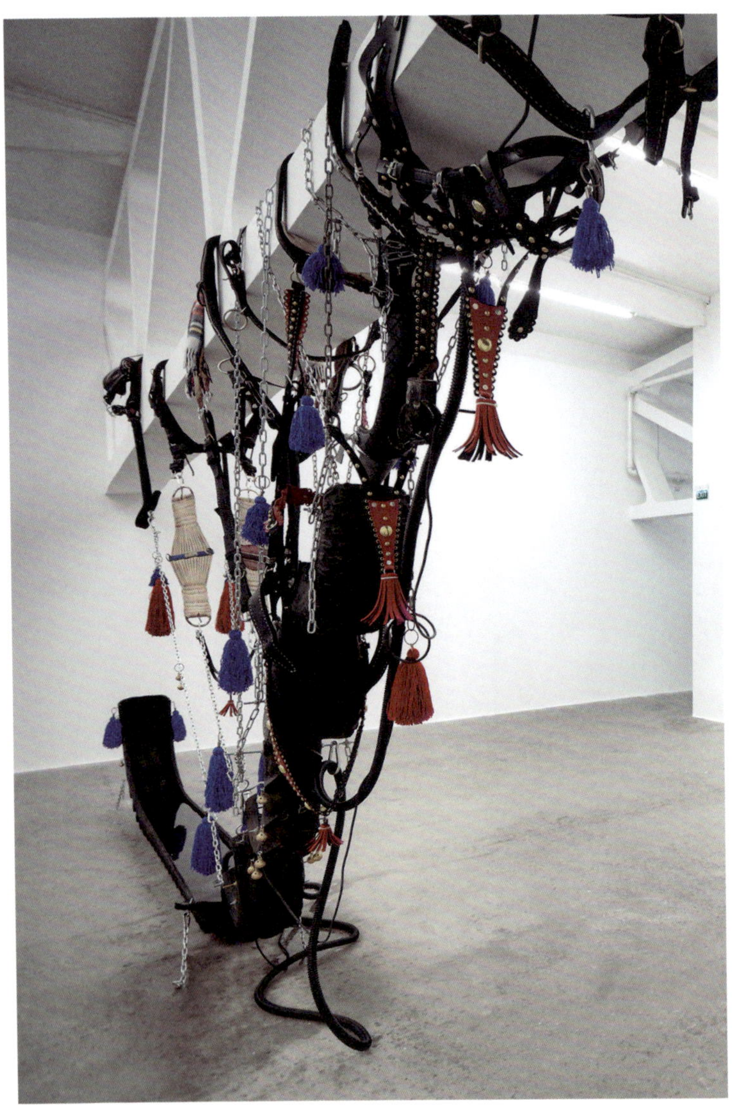

All Animals are Welcome, 2021
tractor tyres, animal chains, horse harnesses, horse
bells, whips, tassels, fountain accesories, water pump

L' Anatomia del Cavallo
Dan Vezentan

28. 05 – 11. 07. 2021

In the first act, the big beam transforms into the spine of a mammal, a possible outsized horse. Then the fountain appears: the tyres of a tractor, plough and seeders are used post-mortem in a waterfall composing a new hydration system. Replaced by technology in the industrial revolution, quadrupeds are now claiming their land. Synthetic troughs are suspended in chains and harnesses, the former means of domestication and control are used against technology – the machine.

The vertebrae are carefully protected by harnesses and soft blankets so that the system's vertebral column is comfortable. The horses dissected in ink[1] are going to drink at night, surely the sound of water and the sleigh bells will hypnotically attract them to the source. The central watering station transforms into an oasis for traction animals while the economic engine needs some refreshment.

The exhibition is a tribute to the horse, an anatomical study of the economic engine, a place of hydration for traction animals.

Dan Vezentan

---

[1] *Anatomia del cavallo, infermità, et suoi rimedii* by Carlo Ruini (Venezia, 1598). The first anatomy textbook dedicated to a species other than man. It represents a reference mark in veterinary / equine publications, it is known due to its sketches which are strongly influenced by the human anatomical works published in the previous decades, especially in *De Fabrica Corporis Humani* (Basel, 1543), by Andreas Vesalius.

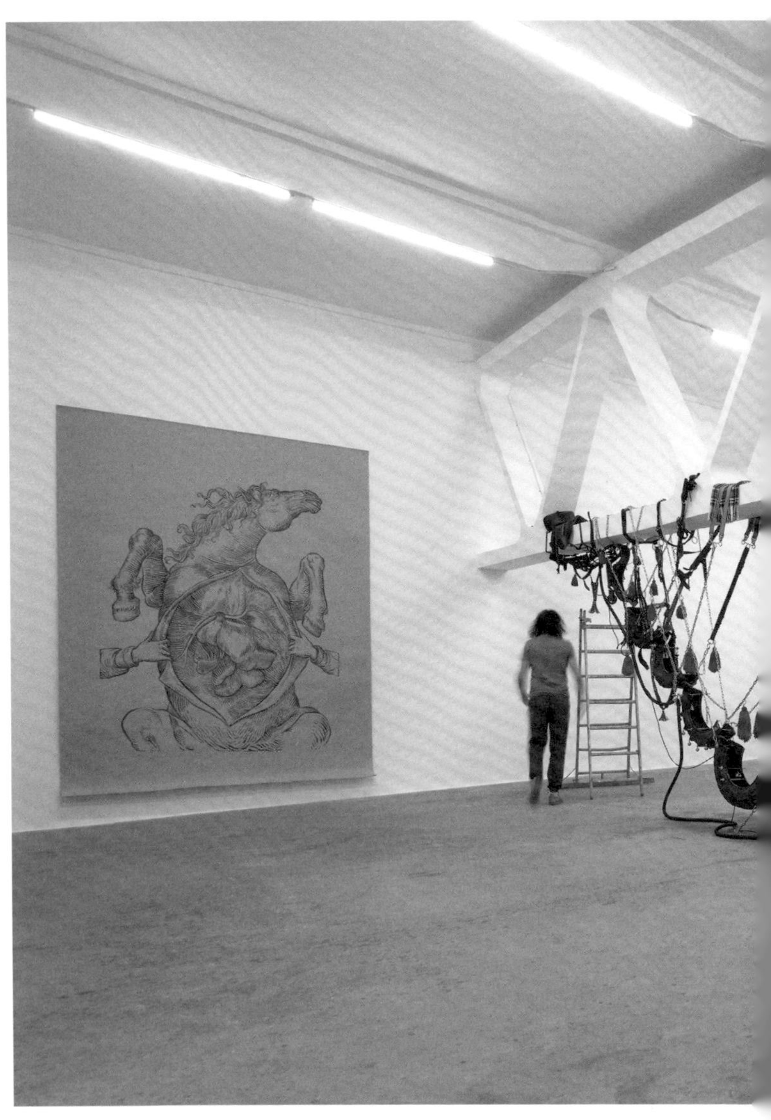

L' Anatomia del Cavallo
exhibition view

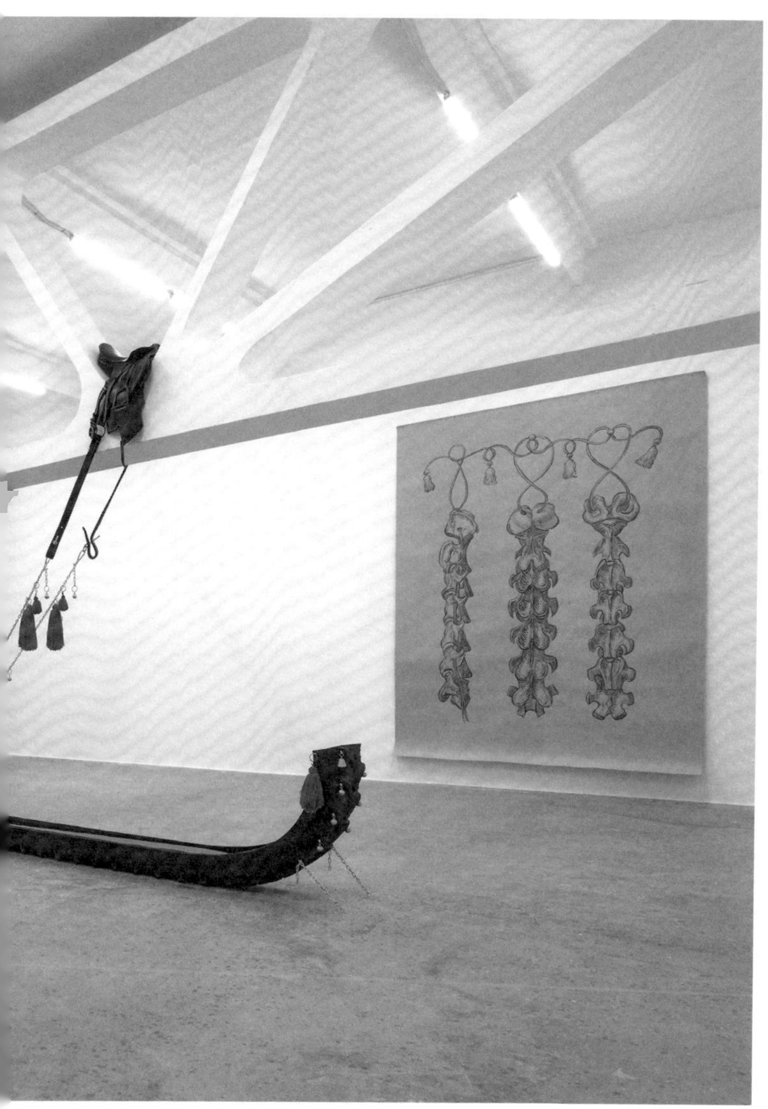

L' Anatomia del Cavallo
exhibition view

next spread

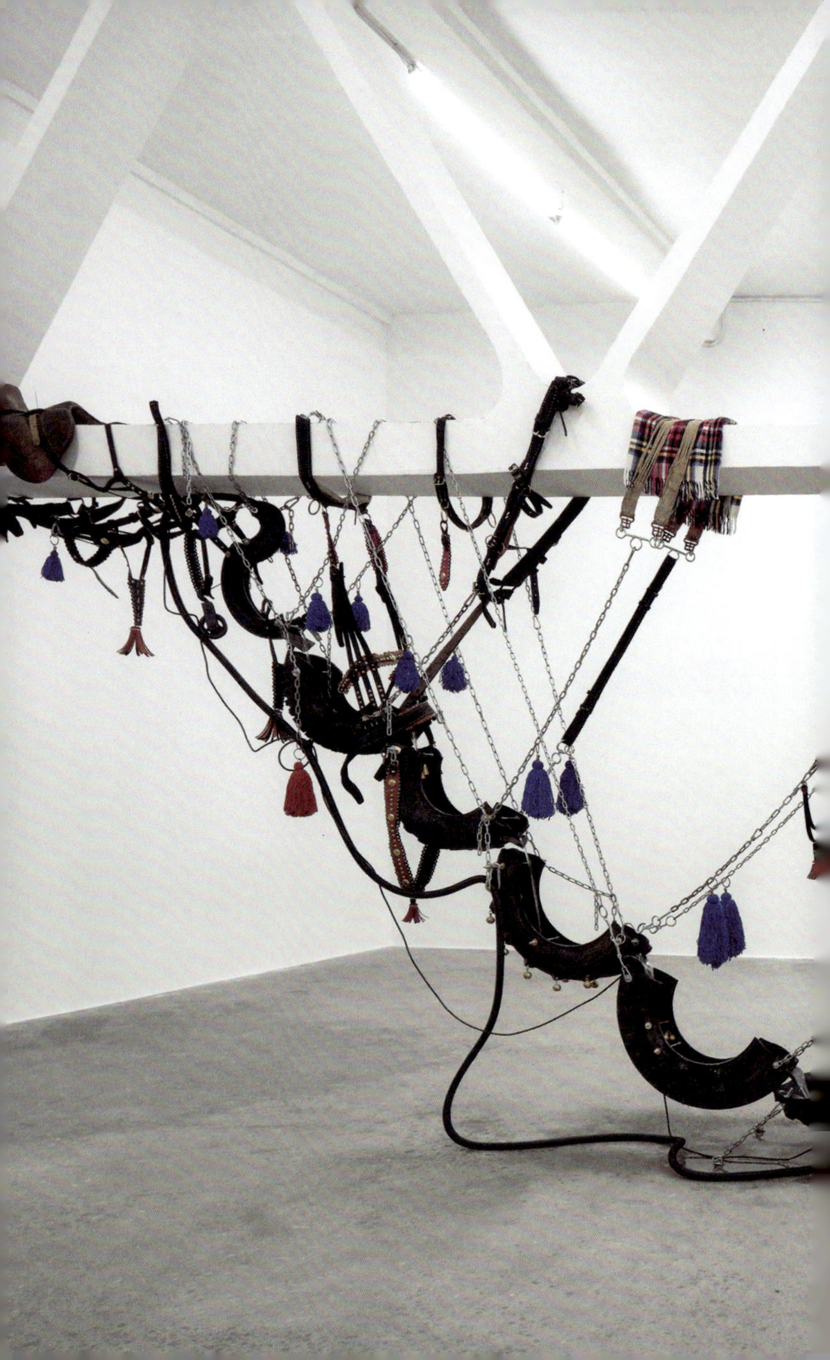

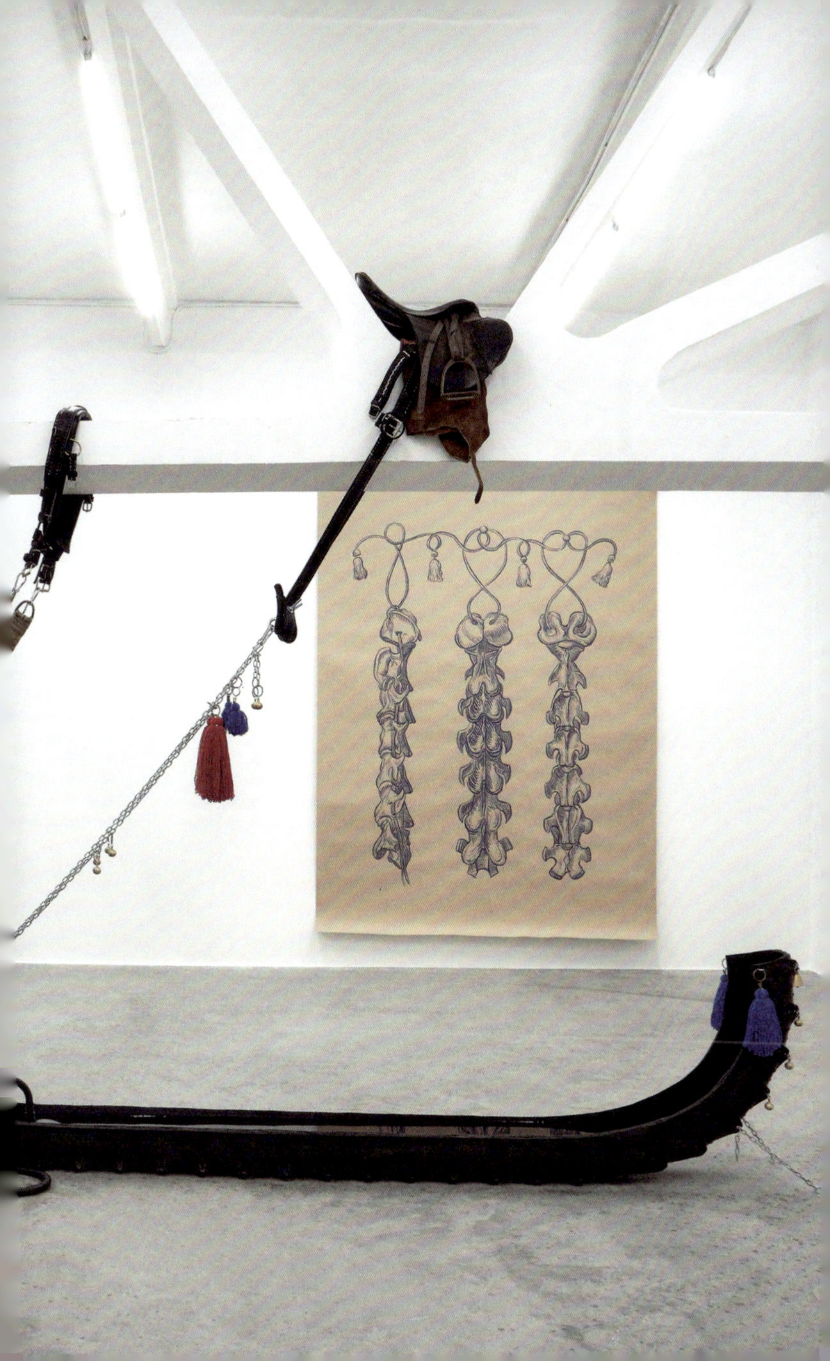

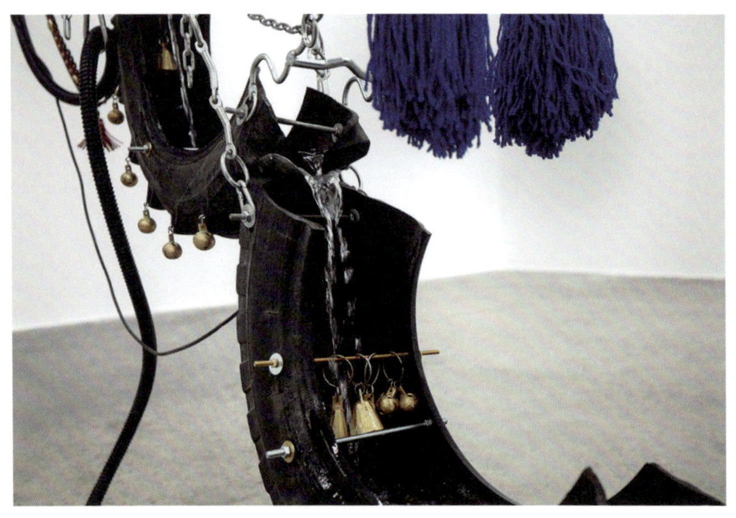

All Animals are Welcome, 2021
tractor tyres, animal chains, horse harnesses, horse
bells, whips, tassels, fountain accesories, water pump
(detail)

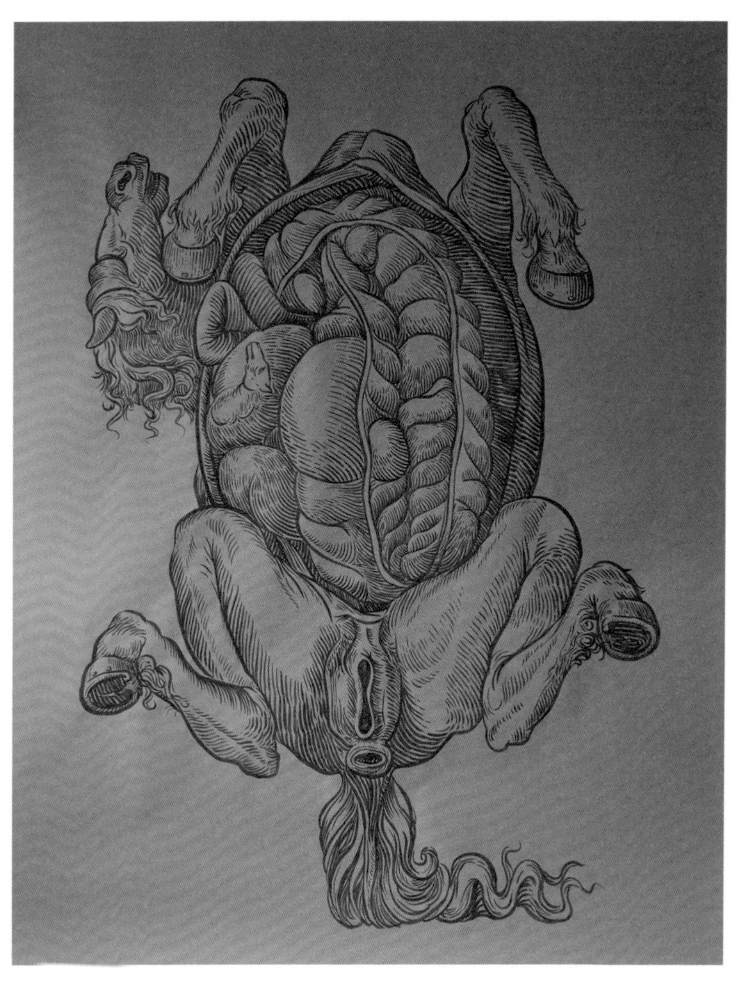

L' Anatomia del Cavallo, Tauola II del Lib. IV, VI, 2019
ink on paper, 270 x 320 cm

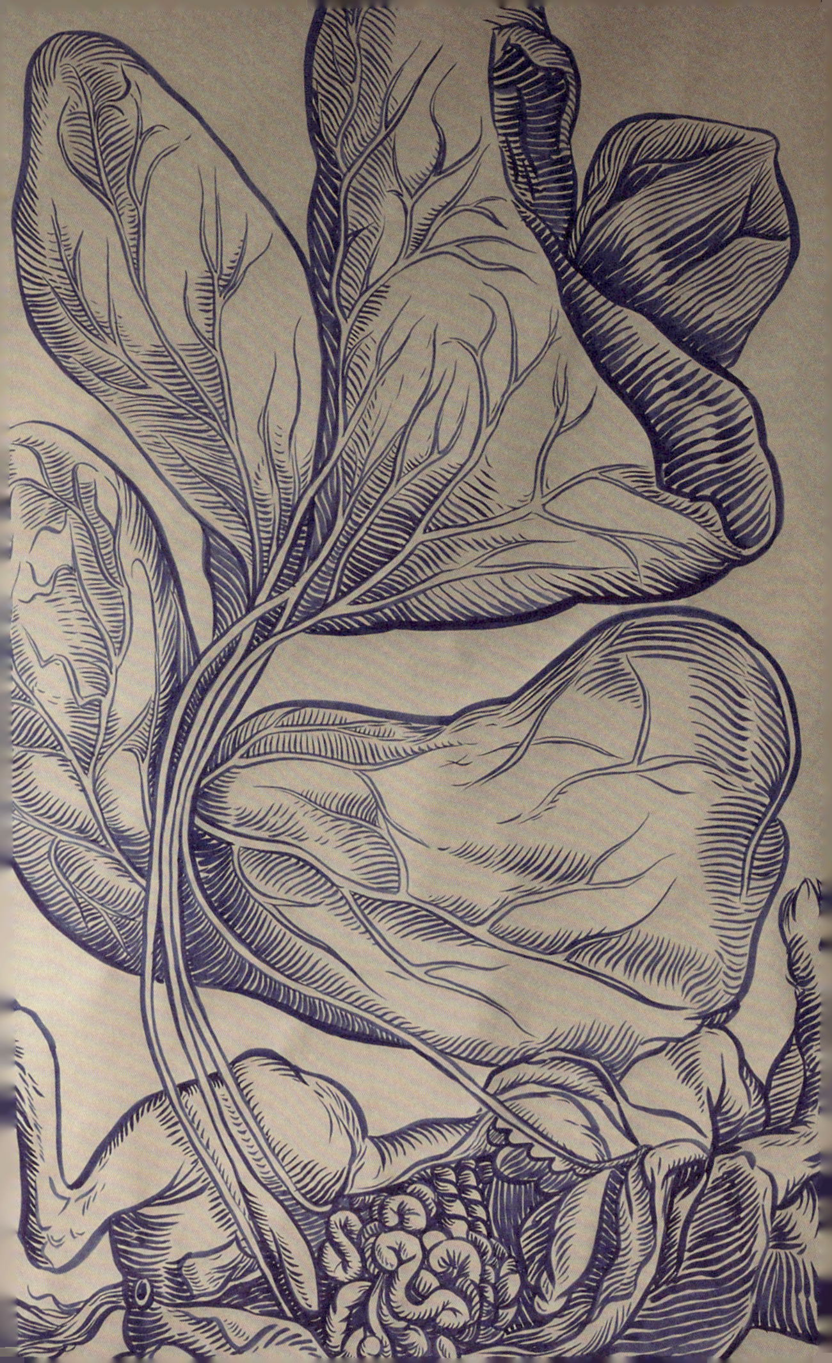

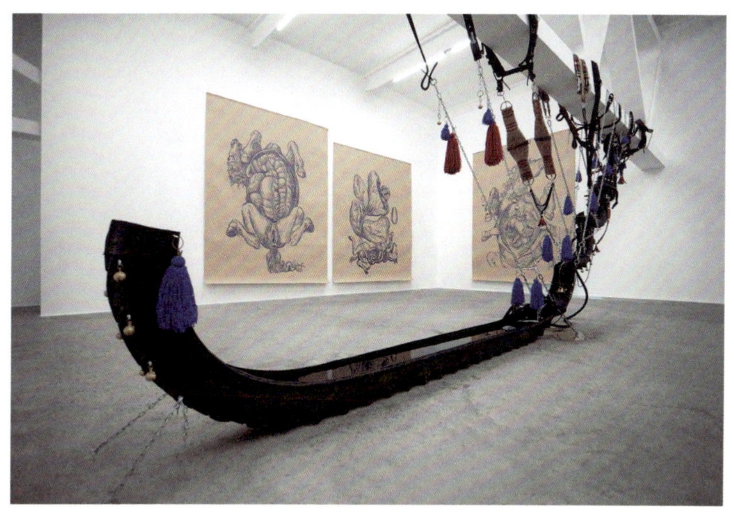

L' Anatomia del Cavallo
exhibition view

L' Anatomia del Cavallo, Tauola II del Lib. IIII, VII, 2019
ink on paper, 270 x 320 cm
(detail)

previous page

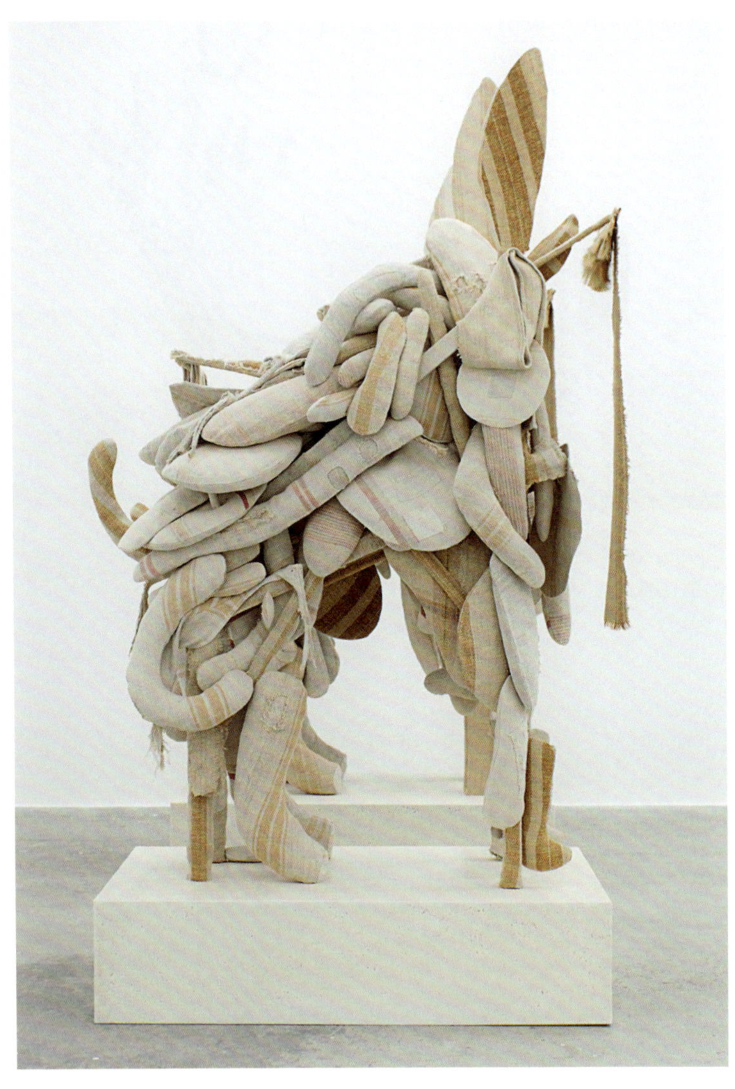

Szénaizmok szalaghegyen
Haystacks on the Mountain of Ribbons
installation views

pages 80 - 87

Szénaizmok szalaghegyen
Haystacks on the Mountain of Ribbons
Oláh Gyárfás

27. 11. 2020 – 24. 01. 2021

Some animals take you to the afterlife. Lunatic. Silent.
Psychopomp. Splints are the ones which guard the
house, the door, privacy itself. The way to his own self,
the way to God, to the sacred world. Domestic, some
animals carry your burden: your body, all that warms
it up and whatever is feeding it. There are some others,
plush toys, porcelain trinkets, small ready-made ones
that stop the tears, replacing the mother's breast and
making the outside world bearable.

Some others are created only by your imagination and
you were the only one who experienced all this.
The creatures of Oláh Gyárfás spend their time opening
and closing a transitional universe[1]. An intermediary
and *potential* place, as Winnicott states, where you
experiment with the idea of autonomy and creativity,
your particular existence. It is a place where you
can play and have fun, which helps you to endure
ruptures, transitions and the idea of otherness, while
compensating the loss of the whole's illusion. There are
archaic, ferocious, disturbing and paradoxical fantasies.

Crocote and Leucrocote[2], Szénaizmok and
Szalaghegyen[3] have fur covered with scales and hay
organs on sight; wolf neck, tail and chest, donkey back,
a mouth stretching to its ears and an unbroken bone
instead of teeth. They have soft and mobile horns,
eyes to the hoof, goat fringes and dog paws, warrior

81

skin bandaged with cloth and could delicately imitate
the human voice. They are made of wood, hemp
cloth, flour and hay, quoi de plus doux? (what could be
gentler?) and their materiality immediately befriends
them. They are domestic (animals).

Like Kafka's guardian, in a short story, *In Front of the Law*,
they take care of a gate. Of one gate only. Of a threshold
which is only yours. Of a promise regarding a journey.
In order to pass beyond, you must become a child again:
to be reborn in a new world, to get to Korowai.

For Oláh Gyárfás, the gate of happiness (which opens on
its own) must be made of flour and water. Like bread.
The gate must be very small, the one who enters has
to bow, not necessarily because of humility, but as a
symbol of passage. In the world beyond you must enter
like a child.

Dana Diminescu

[1] D.W. Winnicott, *Transitional Objects and Transitional Phenomena – A Study of the First Not-Me Possession* in: International Journal of Psycho-Analysis, 1953, 34:89-97

[2] Crocote and Leucrocote are imaginary beings described by Ctesias, Artaxerxes Mnemon's doctor. Borges refers to him when citing Pliny (VIII, 3°) in his book published at the Polirom Publishing House, 2006, p. 263.

[3] *Szénaizmok* and *Szalaghegyen*, translated as *Haystacks and On the Mountain of Ribbons*.

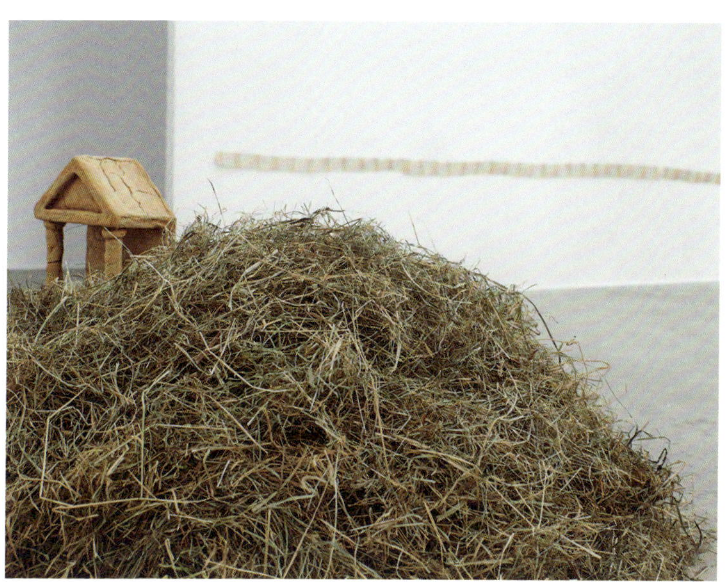

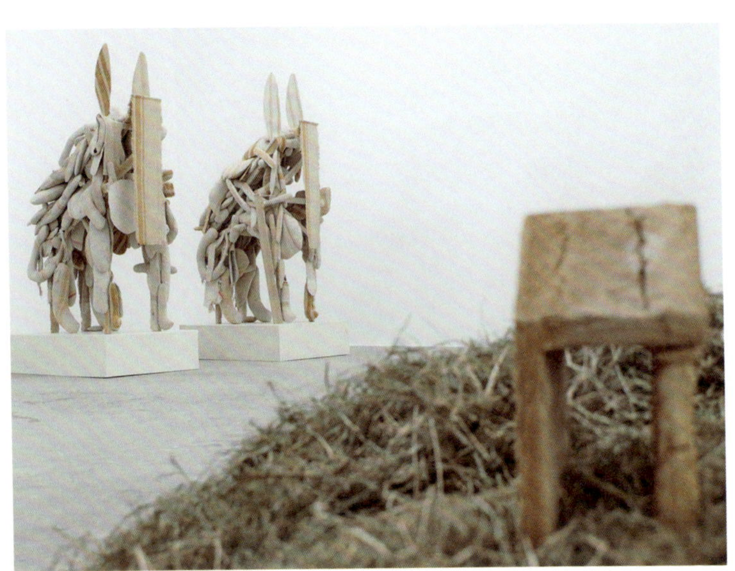

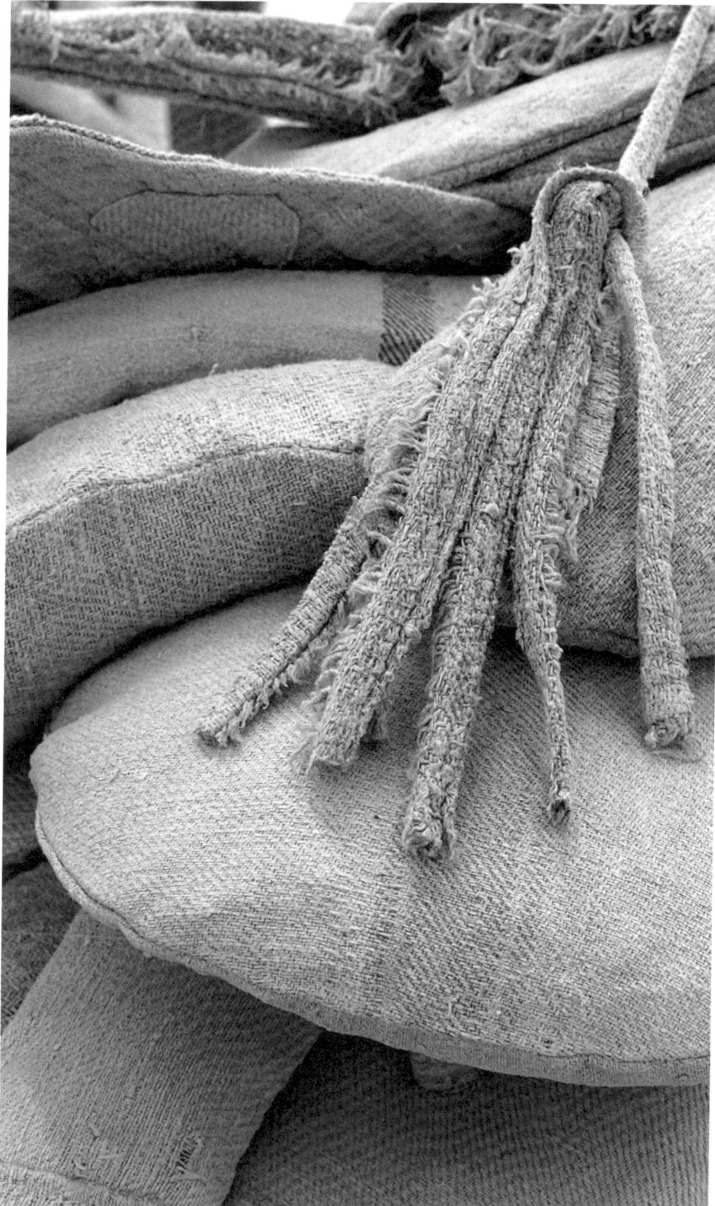

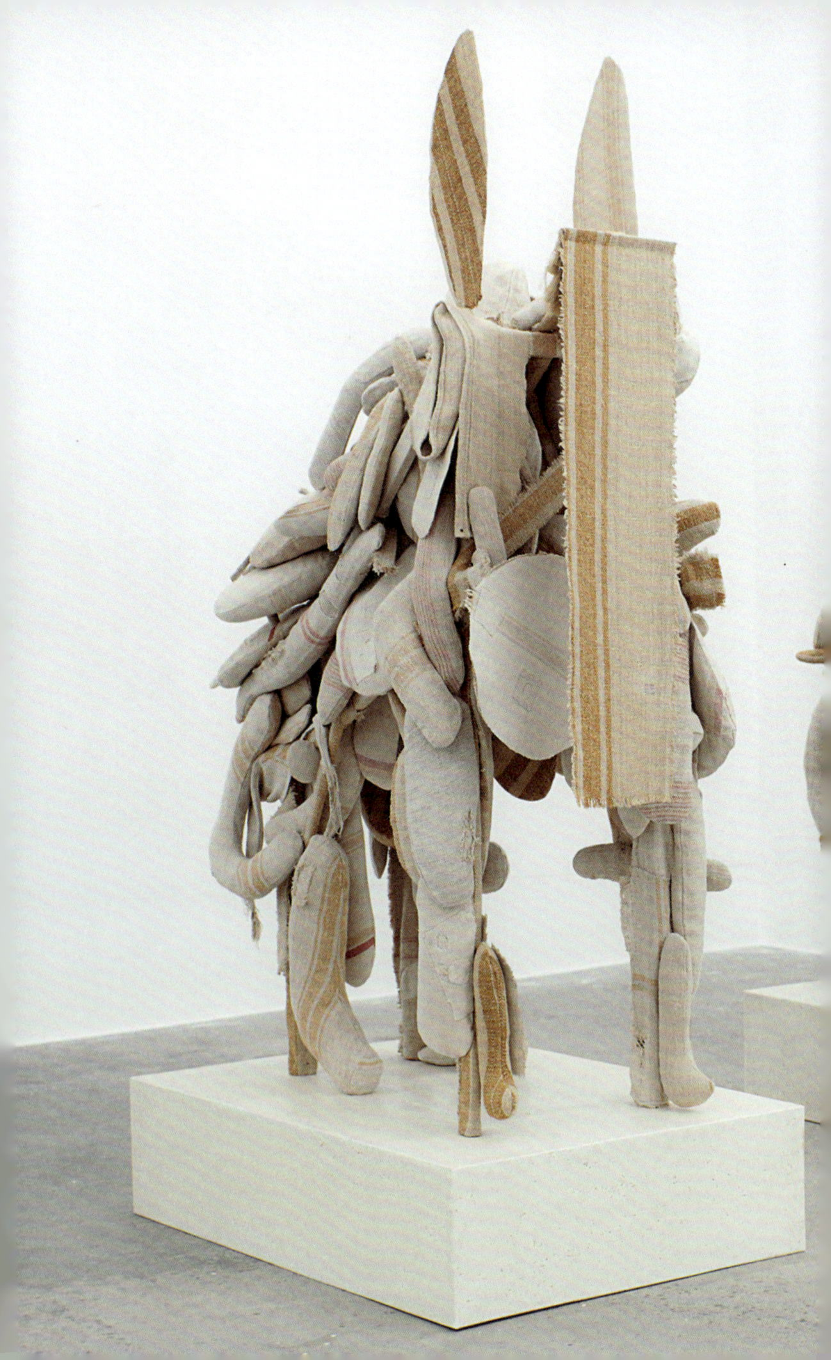

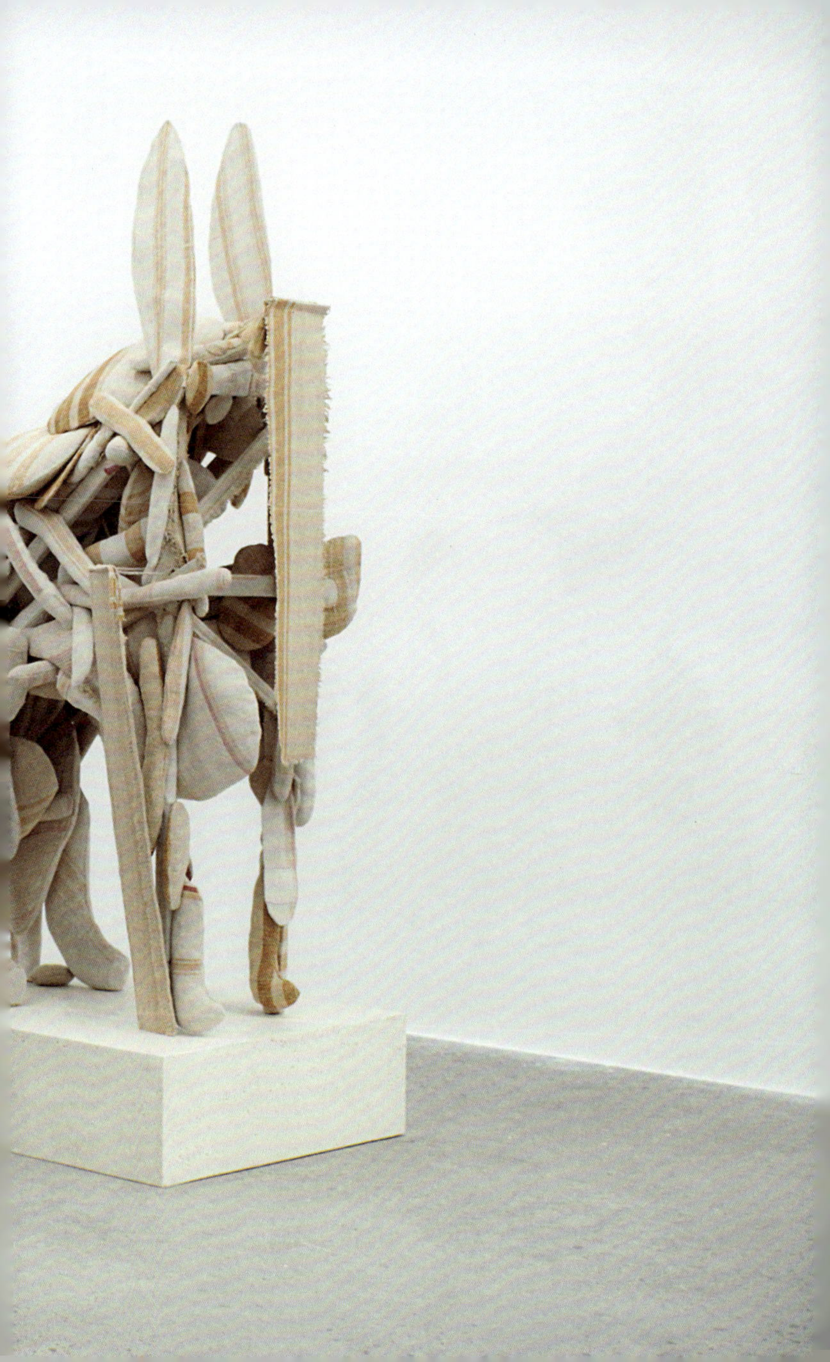

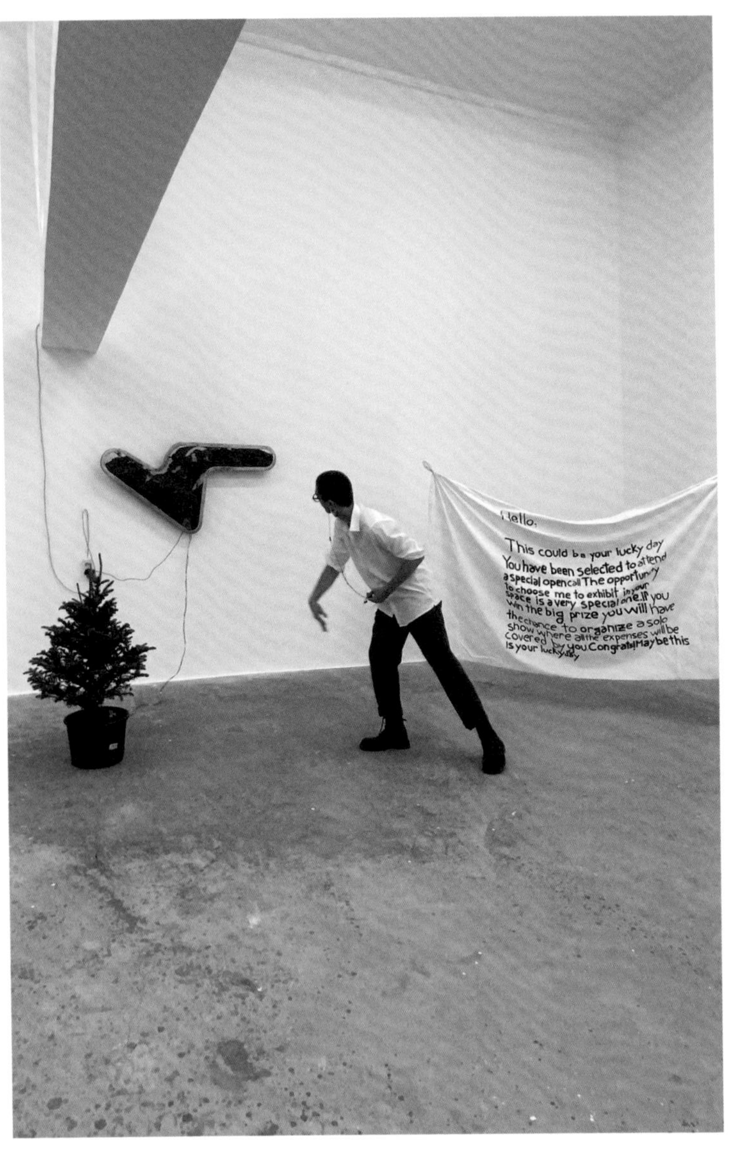

Later Edit
exhibition view

Later Edit
Gavril Pop
Teo Papadopol
Ana Maria Szöllösi
Nicoló Filippo Rosso
Tijana Kačarević
Lera Kelemen
George Roșu
Adrian Oncu
Dorian Bolca
Miki Velciov
Bogdan Matei
Ioana Terheș
Dreaming About my Unborn Child Group:
Alexandra Satmari, Dona Arnakis,
Elena Langă, Ana Maria Szöllösi,
Oana Sas, Loredana Ilie, Ludmila Naghi,
Maria Ungureanu, Alma Gyovai,
Mihaela Vilău, Gabriela Roșca,
Sânziana Gheorghe, Vivien Fritz

17. 10 – 20. 11. 2020
curator: Maria Orosan-Telea

The *Later Edit* exhibition reunites the thirteen projects
carried out under the Draft Curatorial Program over
two years, emphasising a curatorial research method
according to which the stages preceding an actual
exhibition are approached as stable moments and, at
the same time, as elements of a fluid itinerary.

Draft began in 2018 as a form of negotiation between
artistic situations in the process of crystallisation
and the solutions of presentation which they could

take at a certain moment of the production process. For many of these projects, *Draft* represented the proper framework to test its functionality in a real confrontation with the public, or to generate the work in its stage as an idea, by means of a collective and participative intervention.

Later Edit resumes all these projects at a later stage of their existence providing a simultaneous image, in a common space, of what has been accumulated in time regarding the concept meant to present artistic ideas in a visual form with an intermediary and uncertain status.

DRAFT (draftcuratorialprogram.ro) is a curatorial program presenting ongoing art projects, ideas and experiments, partially completed projects or larger-scale replicable samples. Conceptualization, research and analysis are the key points in identifying the appropriate format for their presentation. Exhibiting ideas or art works at intermediate stages questions the vague boundaries between the creative process and the definitive work. The aim is to make a frame stop in an ongoing conceptual structure.

Interaction with the public becomes a generative premise and can have a determined role in increasing or changing the trajectory of the future project. Our desire is to create a context of contiguity and free discussion, in which the transmitter and receiver constantly change their roles.

Maria Orosan-Telea

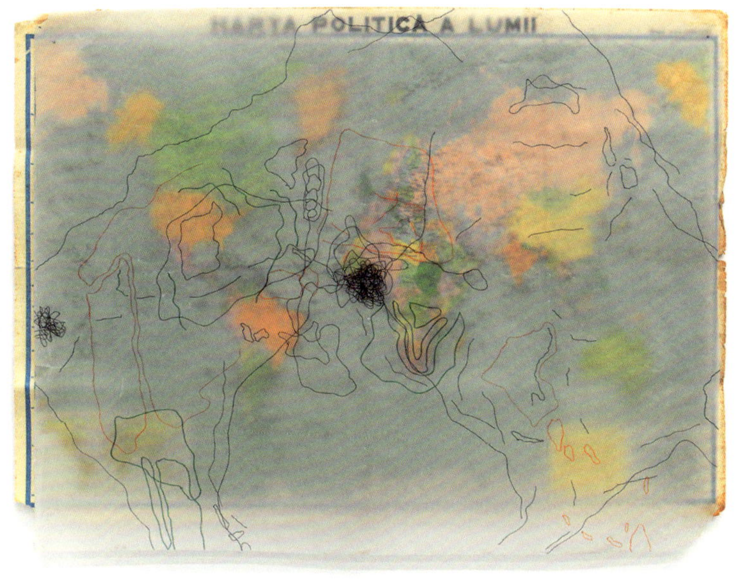

Ana Maria Szöllősi, *The Map*, 2019
map, tracing paper, marker
variable dimensions

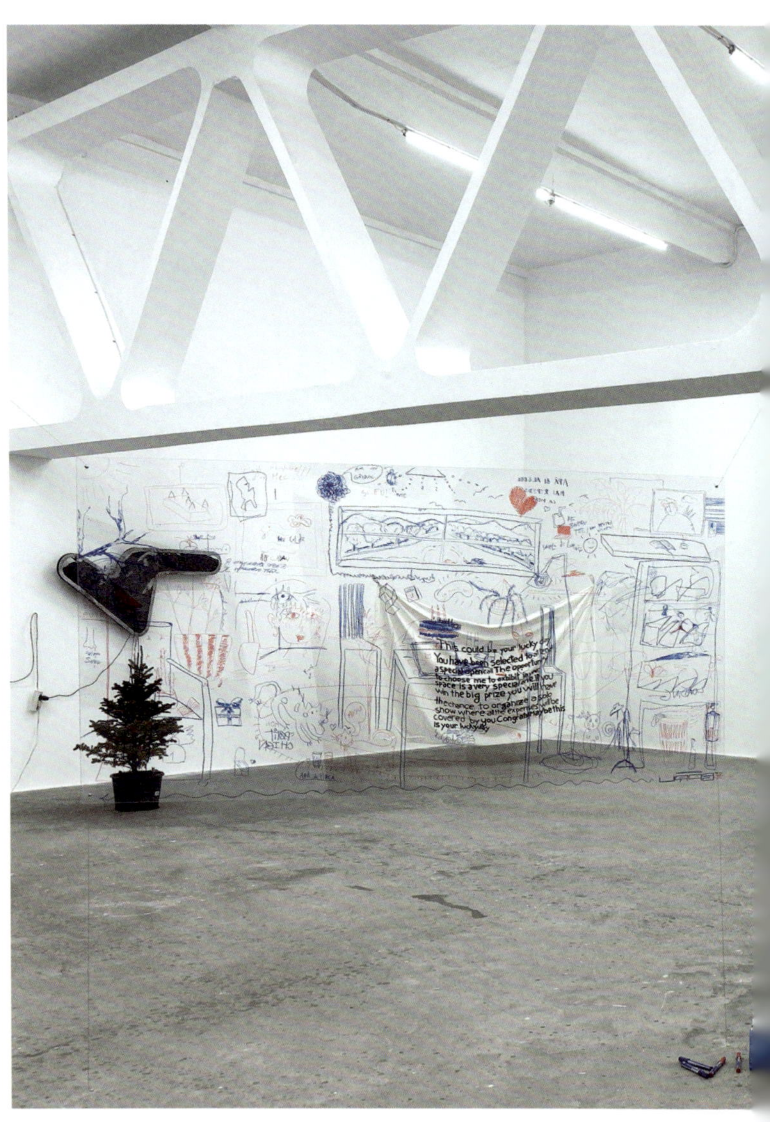

Later Edit
exhibition view

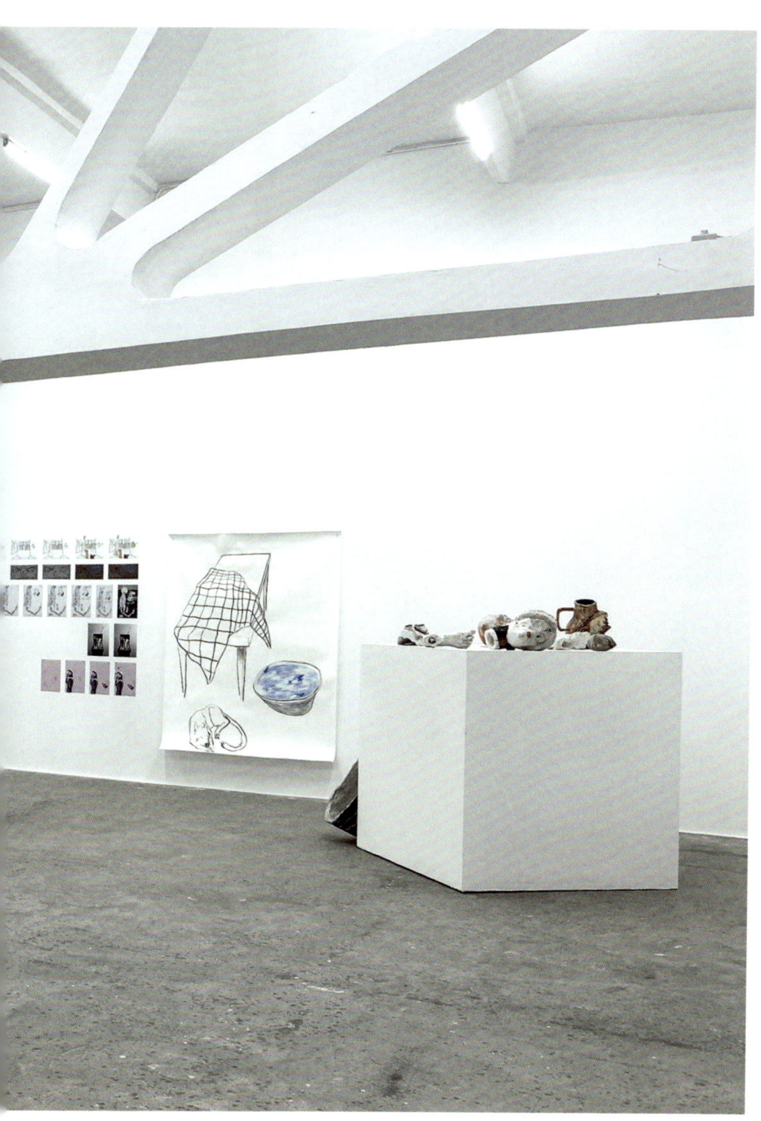

Gavril Pop, *Wiped Out*, 2018
note books, metal board, magnets, 200 x 100 cm
next spread

Dinou la scoala

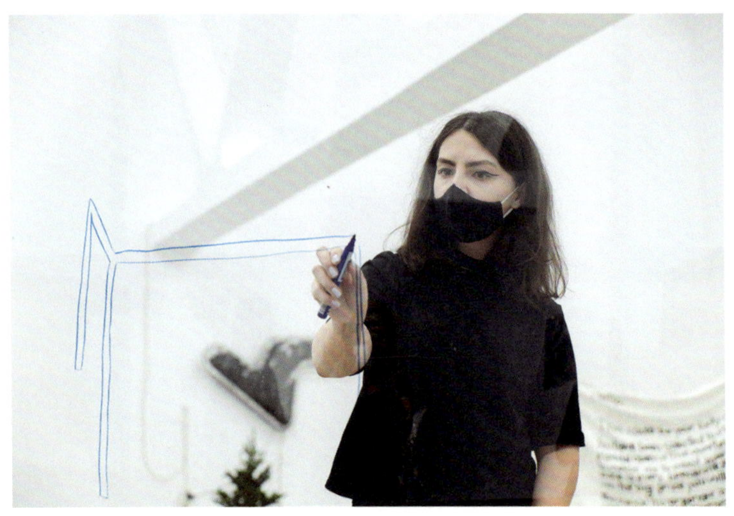

Ioana Terheș, *Public Privacy*, 2020
drawing performance

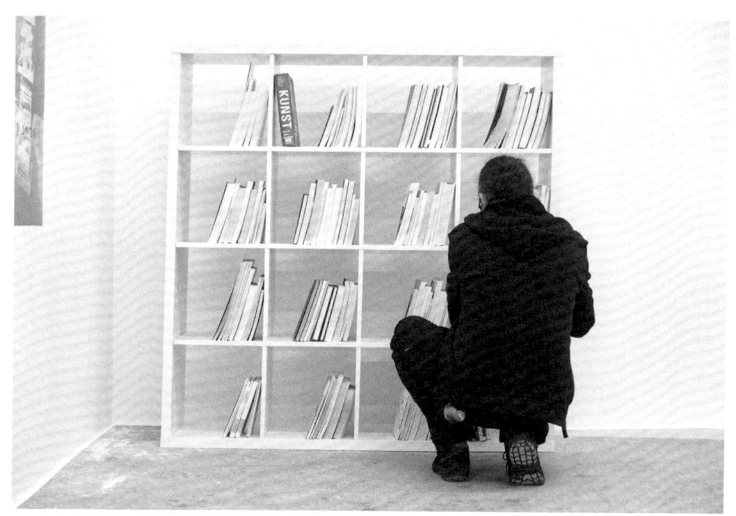

George Roșu, *Instuctions for Reversing Books*, 2020
performance

Later Edit
exhibition view
next spread

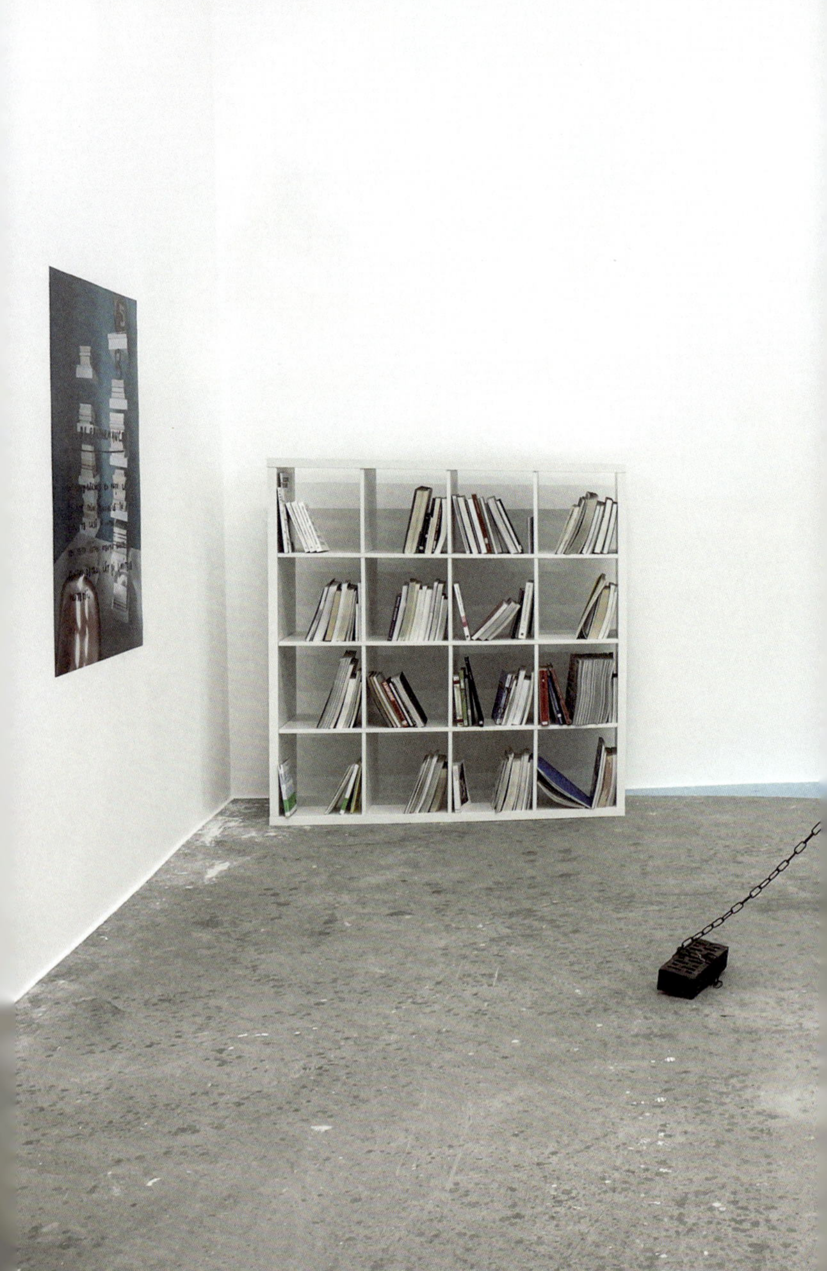

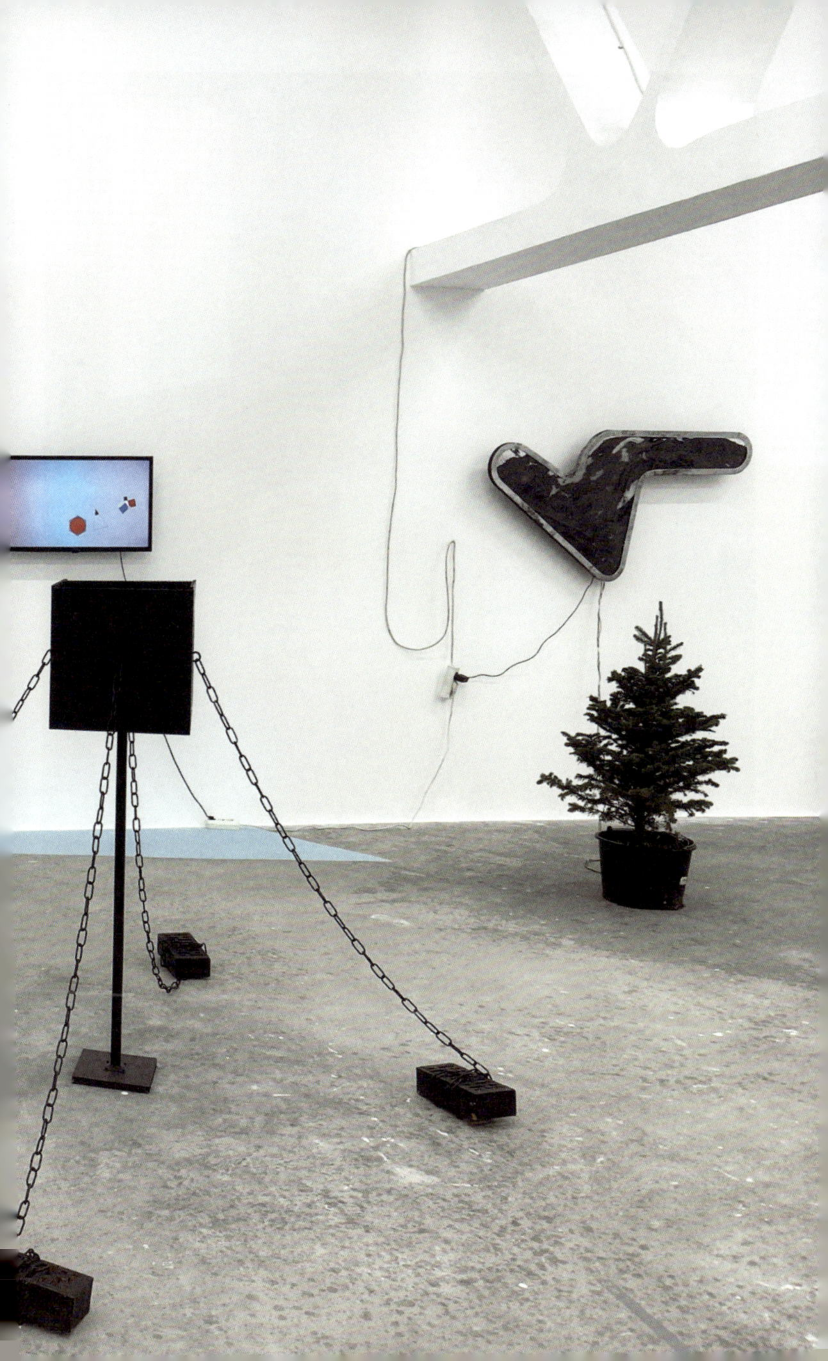

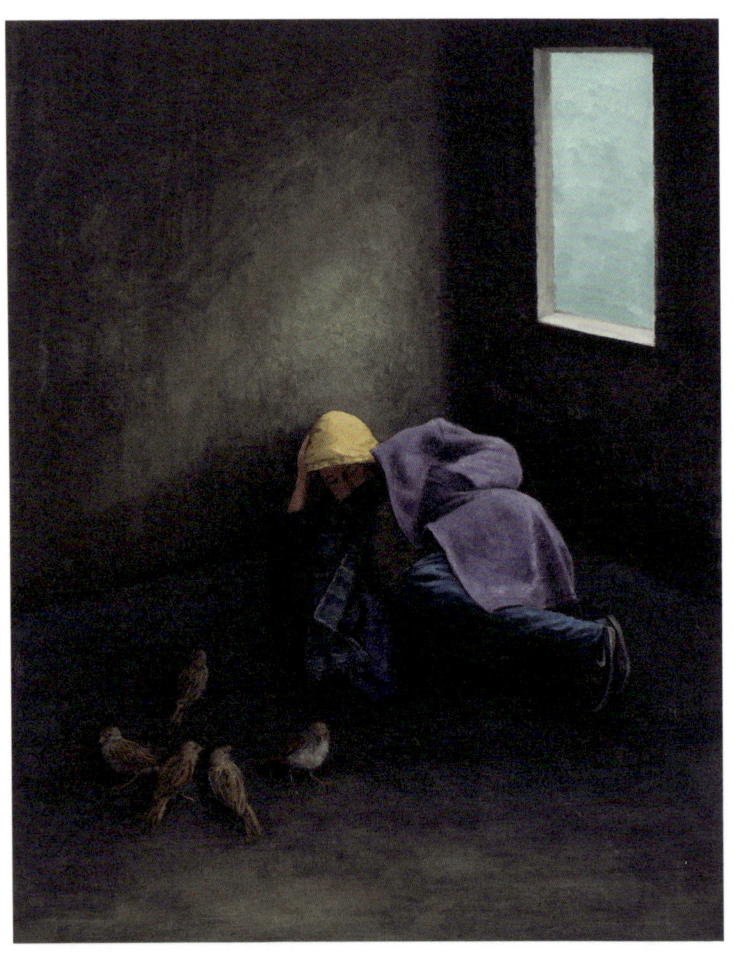

The Antechamber, 2016
oil on canvas, 98 x 78 cm

Equinox
Șerban Savu

20. 03 – 20. 05. 2020
curator: Mihai Pop

Preamble.
An innocent parlor game, when the year turned
around, showed me what I was meant to live this year:
the difficult moment of the battle between day and
night, the point suggesting the most intense fragility
which the forces of nature were coping with. In my
choice, the card tells that, on such a day, in China,
people stay indoors, sheltered from the calendar's
demons, while the dual energies of nature at the time
of the spring equinox are so powerful and frightening.

Penumbra. The painting.
There is a latent dimension in the painting of Șerban
Savu, which is always there, yet it is never clarified,
not even in the interviews provided by the artist over
the years. And its emphasis implies a persevering
view, issued not only by the search for the anecdotical
detail, but also by the references of art history (briefly,
the deactivation of knowledge regarding Savu's
work). This exercise demands the careful research
of the canvas, over and over again, while focusing
on the penumbra, on the "residual" surfaces of the
image, which are always there as the necessary
balance of the painted subject. Savu's characters
are also connected to the penumbra, they are also
suspended, continuously, in a space expressing the
potential of an action, but one which is dropping
off, anticipating the release of "reality." These

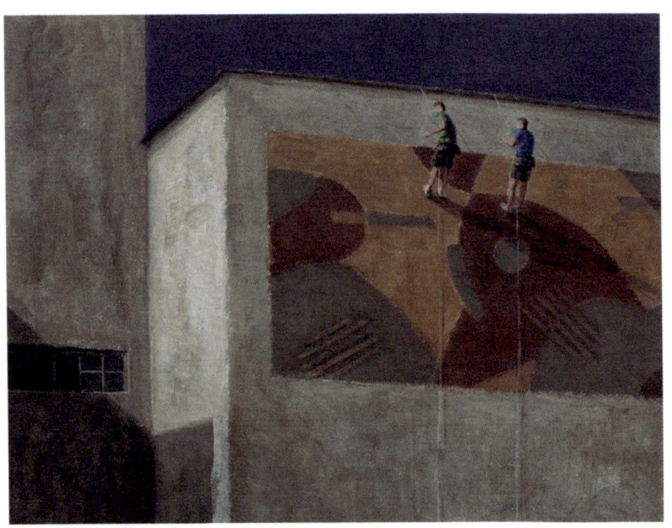

Abstract Composition, 2019
oil on canvas, 30 x 40 cm

characters are rather defined through the connection
with the flow of nature (hibernation, expectation,
germination), and less by their role in the "social
scene" (and, by extension, in the economy of the
work). Although the nature painted by Savu is mostly
artificial, subordinated to architecture and adapted to
characters, the relationship between man and nature
represents the inward subject of his paintings, which
is never told, written or described. This relationship of
interdependence is the humane characteristic latently
suggested by his painting.

The painting. The exhibition.
What can the painting do in the best way? In our case,
to preserve the parts' fragile balance unbroken.

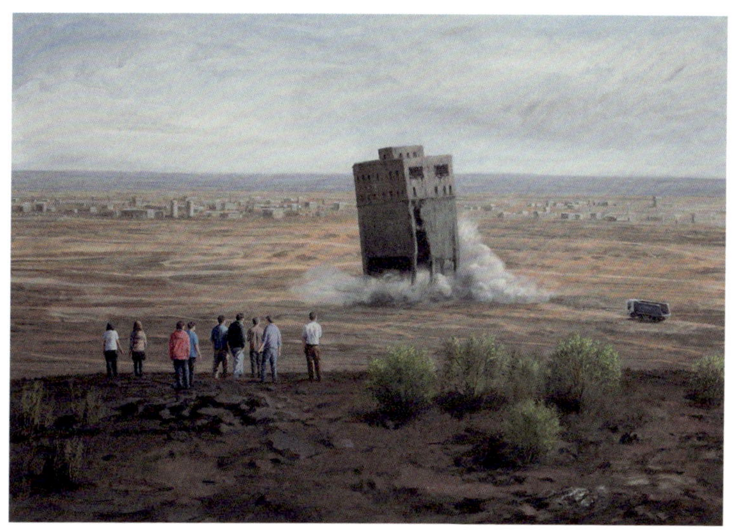

Random Audience, 2014
oil on canvas, 134 x 192 cm

And we shall find ourselves in it only so far as the
ambiguity of this pressure is reflected, far from the
falsehood of some simplifying certainty. That is why
we keep looking at it, as it comprises the obscurity,
which is so important, the compost, which nourishes
us. The paintings carry their penumbra within
themselves and, as a whole, the exhibition is also the
carrier of such fertile uncertainty. Seen from this
viewpoint, the exhibition becomes the antidote of a
mercantile stimulus in the overproduction of actual
art. One more reason to open it at the time of the
spring equinox. Thus, the painting carrying
the penumbra is provided with clarity, showing
up in the most appropriate moment, due to our
capacity to carefully concentrate on the painting's

dusky zone. In art, the transition from "winter" to "spring" is done through this hard and concentrated process of the view.

The exhibition. The shadow.
Until the spring equinox, when, on March 20th, the painting and its reception in the exhibition are going to get equal rights, the discoursive temptation is to equalise the construction of the exhibition with the way from the germinative darkness to the light itself. The point marking the perfect balance between day and night emphasises the exceptional state of the reflexive context created by the exhibition. This is possible as Șerban Savu naturally assumes to approach the metaphor in his creation. Thus, we found it natural to name and open the exhibition on the day of the equinox.

Addendum.
During the student years, every spring I used to travel from the grey and gloomy Cluj to the Student Fest from Timișoara, which was overflowing with vitality. Everything was related to the idea of commencement and renewal. However, the exhibition we used to always prepare together, while sensing the overflowing spring, was invariably set up with and about the dark side of each of us. A condition which was both fragile and fertile, to preserve - no matter which the practice of every one of us was - the melancholy and shadow.

Mihai Pop

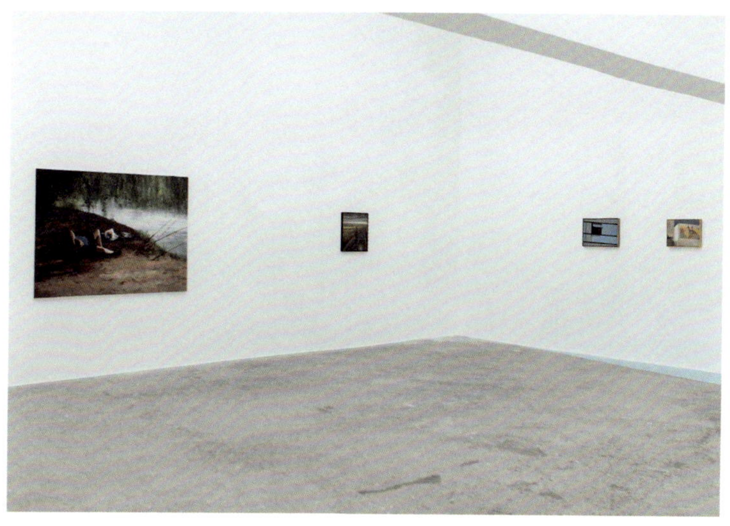

Equinox
exhibition view

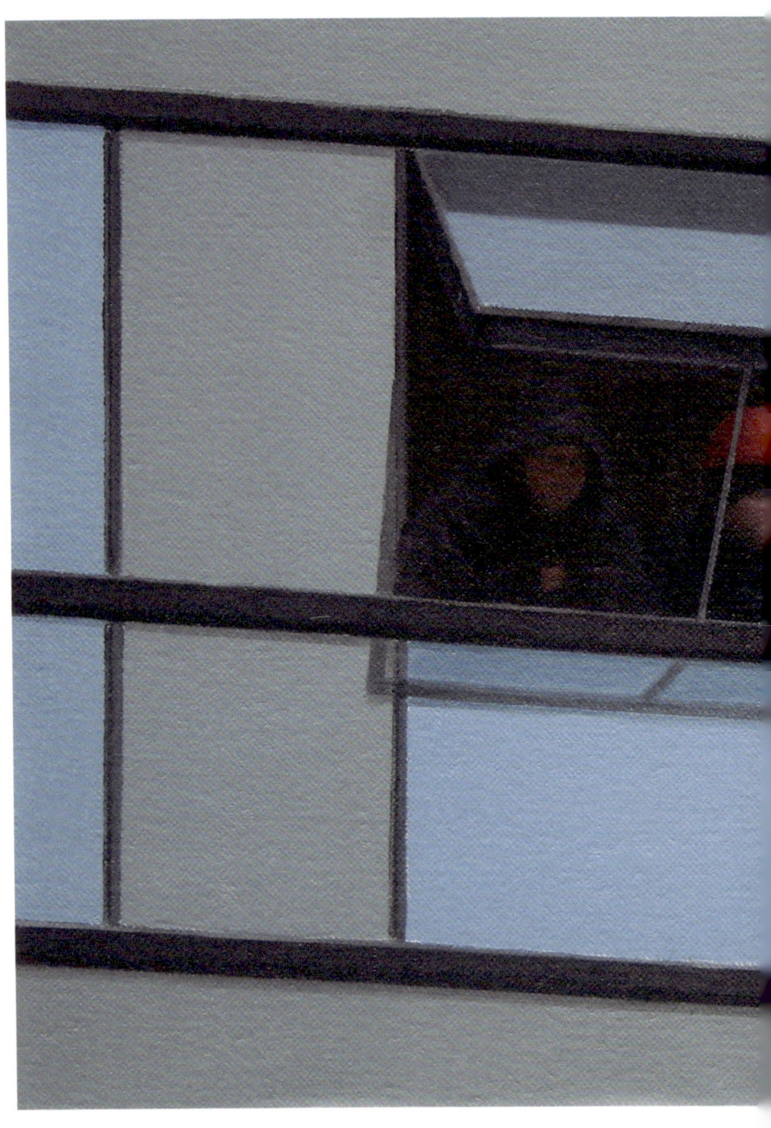

Untitled, 2006
oil on canvas, 33 x 50 cm

Equinox, exhibition view

next spread

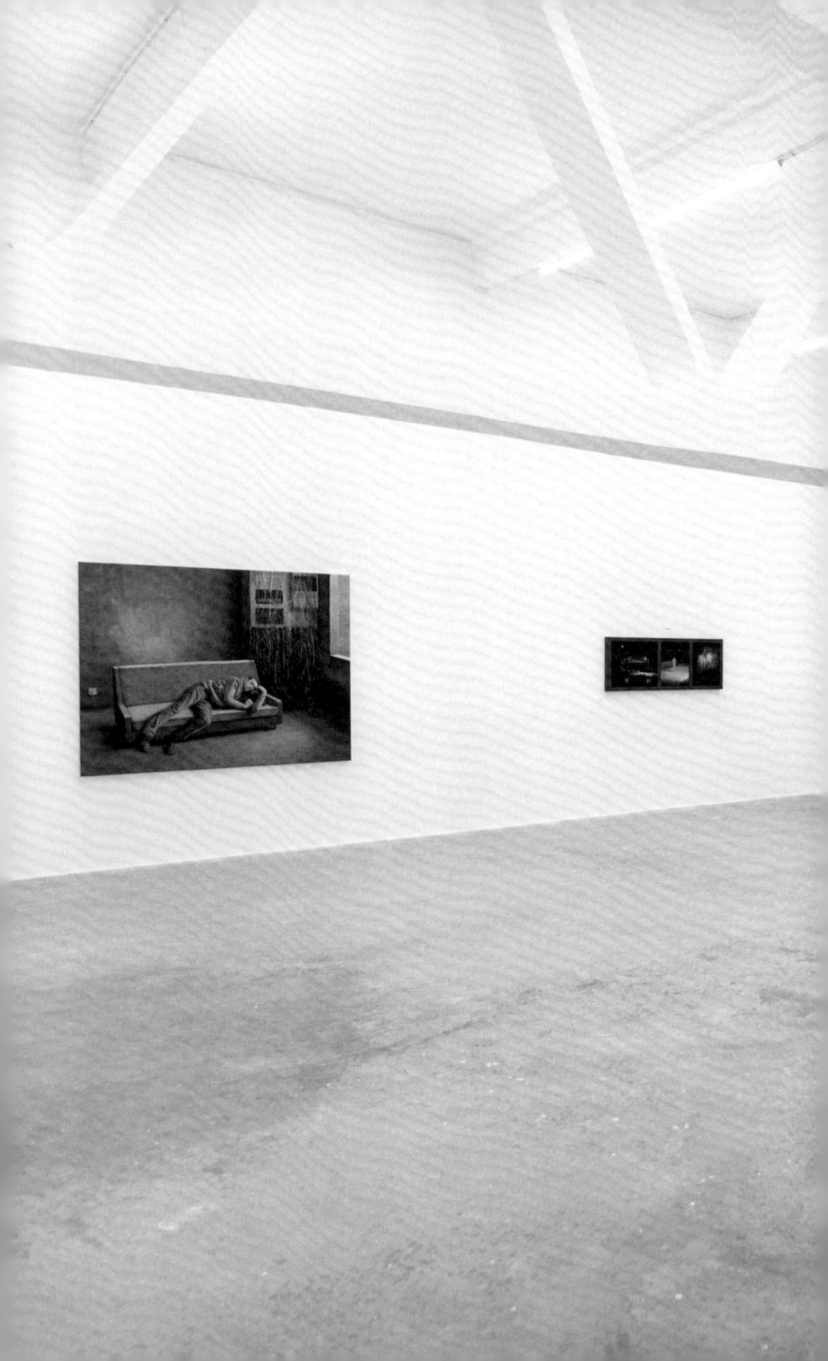

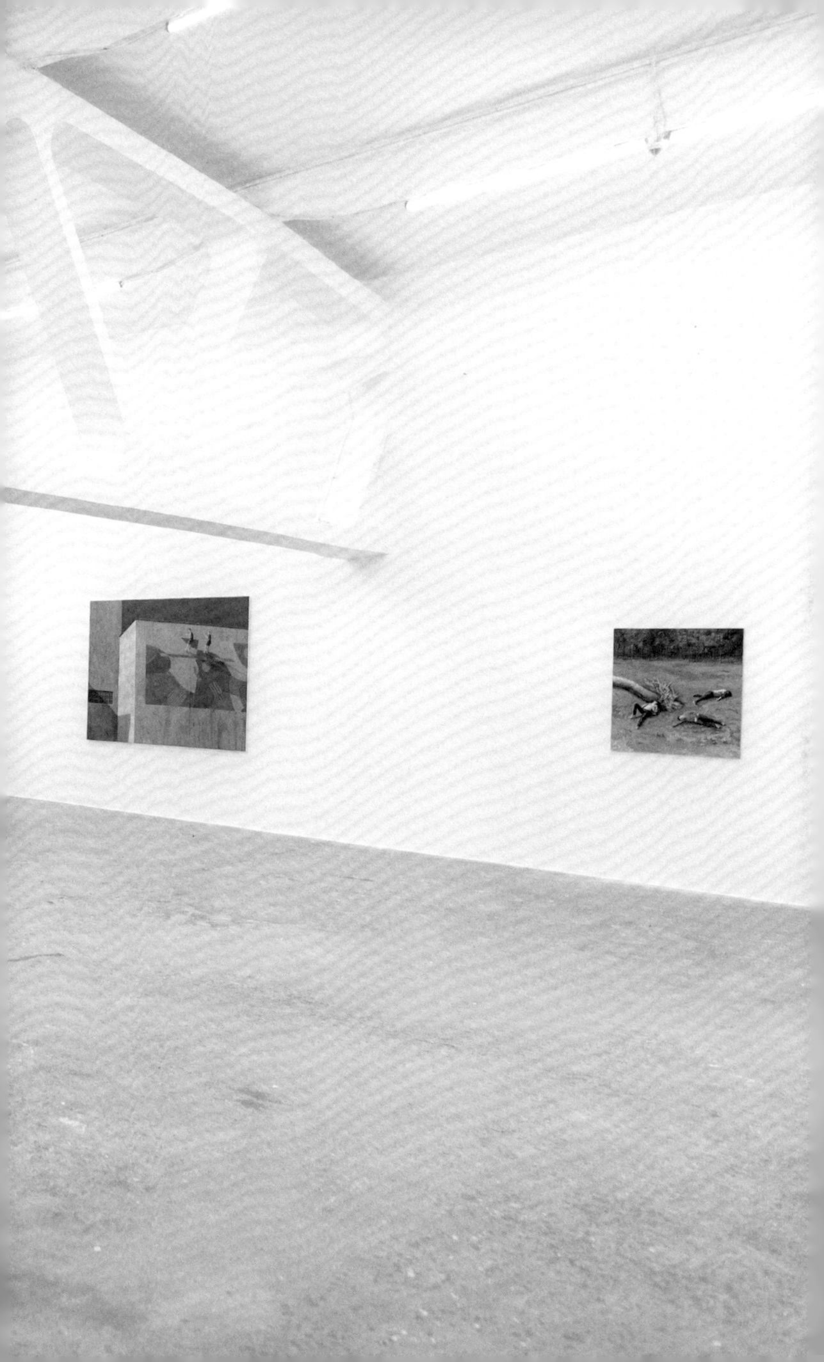

Texts in Romanian **/ Texte în română**

Cuprins

Planul
Anca Verona Mihuleț

Modul în care percepem spațiile de intersecție și interacțiune este determinat de un complex de elemente, variind de la practici senzoriale personale sau colective la percepția materiei și la factori psihologici. Fie că vorbim despre muzeu sau despre galerie, spațiul expozițional ține de categoria spațiilor de intersecție și interacțiune, împreună cu alte forme spațiale, precum magazinul universal, așa cum l-a descris Walter Benjamin, sau strada, așa cum a fost imaginată de situaționiști. Diversele posibilități de prezentare a „lucrurilor" sunt menite să definească experiențele zilnice sau pe termen lung și să le redea în forme atipice care ar putea complica percepția, ridica întrebări sau atrage observatorul într-un joc ontologic.

Istoria expunerii artei într-un regim care să reflecte atât experiența privitorului, cât și atitudinea instituției, oferind în același timp o prezentare vibrantă și contextuală a artiștilor, datează de la începutul secolului al XX-lea; exemple notabile și bine documentate provin din Germania, unde Hugo von Tschudi, mai întâi ca director al Galeriei Naționale din Berlin și mai târziu al Neue Pinakothek din München, a propus metode alternative, diferențiate, de a expune impresioniști francezi sau artiști germani. În timpul Republicii de la Weimar, activitatea grupului de gânditori și practicieni din jurul Bauhaus a creat un sistem de reprezentare a tuturor formelor de artă în fața publicului în cel mai funcțional și rațional mod posibil – de la arhitectura specifică până la planurile de proiectare.

În 1939, la cea de-a 10-a aniversare a Muzeului de Artă
Modernă din New York, care a coincis cu inaugurarea
noii sale clădiri proiectate de arhitectul Philip L.
Goodwin, Alfred Barr a curatoriat expoziția *Art in Our
Time* [*Arta în timpul nostru*], o plasare democratică în
spațiu a artei europene și americane, prezentând
picturi, sculpturi, materiale tipărite, fotografii,
filme, artă populară și chiar pictură pentru copii. A
fost un proiect îndrăzneț care a înfățișat „Muzeul
de Artă Modernă ca fiind un laborator: publicul este
invitat să participe în experimentele sale"[1]. Laborator
– experiment – public – interacțiune – atât de bine
reunite într-o declarație la sfârșitul introducerii
curatoriale a lui Barr în catalogul expoziției, deși
aranjamentul lucrărilor de artă a fost considerat
conservator de unii critici. Totuși, această formulă
cvadruplă va deveni relevantă pentru majoritatea
organizatorilor de expoziții în următoarea jumătate a
secolului și mai departe.

Charlotte Klonk, în cartea sa fundamentală *Spaces of
Experience: Art Gallery Interiors from 1800 to 2000* [*Spații
ale experienței: Interioare de galerie din 1800 până în
2000*], susține: „cubul alb nu a existat niciodată. Este
adevărat că erau pereți albi în galeria de artă – au fost
introduși în muzeele germane în anii 1930, preluați de
Muzeul de Artă Modernă din New York și răspândiți
în galerii din toată lumea occidentală – dar conceptul
de a oferi muzeelor pereți de un alb uniform nu a fost
niciodată despre crearea unui spațiu închis, asemenea
unui cub. Pereții albi aveau scopul, mai degrabă, de a
da impresia unui spațiu deschis, în creștere, flexibil și
maleabil."[2]

Adaptabilitatea, reconversia și practicile creative
sunt caracteristici ale apariției spațiilor de artă
în România postrevoluționară. Inițiativele și conceptele
curatorilor și artiștilor reprezintă fundalul istoriei
spațiilor expoziționale, acestea fiind supuse unui proces
mai accelerat în comparație cu politicile culturale
regionale mai puțin progresiste.

Timișoara nu face excepție. În 2019, a fost inaugurată
Kunsthalle Bega; fondatorii săi, Alina Cristescu, Liviana
Dan și Bogdan Rața, au pornit de la ideea cubului
alb privit ca spațiu utopic și au decis să transforme o
parte dintr-o clădire industrială emblematică într-o
„Kunsthalle". Clădirea este un simbol al Timișoarei, fiind
una dintre locațiile în care au avut loc primele proteste
împotriva dictaturii comuniste în decembrie 1989.
Stilul arhitectural al construcției, finalizat la începutul
anilor 1950, este intimidant prin aspectul impunător –
designul particular al clădirii cere reacție, este imposibil
să-l ignori.

Un teoretician abil și atemporal al spațiilor, Siegfried
Kracauer, a afirmat: „imaginile spațiale sunt visele
societății. Acolo unde pot fi descifrate hieroglifele
acestor imagini, se găsește baza realității sociale."[3]
Kracauer a identificat două tipuri de imagini spațiale
care trebuie urmărite: în primul rând, sunt cele care
sunt „formate conștient" și pot fi găsite în planuri și
ghiduri, iar în al doilea rând, există cele considerate a
fi „creații inopinante" – configurații de clădiri, străzi și
figuri cu care se confruntă individul.[4] Kunsthalle Bega se
încadrează în cea de-a doua categorie. Straturi de istorie
și detalii arhitecturale – sistemul de iluminat și prizele
sunt invizibile în spațiu, punând astfel în evidență

elementele de construcție esențiale - împreună cu urmele expozițiilor și proiectelor trecute, oferă o perspectivă asupra orașului. Ampla sală de expoziții ascunde însă și un spațiu metaforic - Kunsthalle Bega Box - a cărui geometrie valorifică proiecte specifice, mai mici, cu o voce puternică.

Box-ul este un loc distinct, o extensie a sălii principale, care poate funcționa ca o galerie tradițională atunci când pereții săi susțin desene sau picturi, ca loc expandabil când delimitează instalații sau ca sală de proiecție când găzduiește lucrări video. Echipa din spatele Kunsthalle Bega se situează la intersecția dintre artele vizuale, istoria artei, jurnalism și literatură și, în consecință, există o abordare multidisciplinară a proiectelor și programelor găzduite în spațiu.

Echinocțiu, prima expoziție care avea să fie deschisă în Kunsthalle Bega Box în 2020, a propus o serie de picturi de Șerban Savu, curatoriată de Mihai Pop, co-fondatorul Galeriei Plan B din Cluj. Concepută inițial pentru a fi prezentată în ziua echinocțiului de primăvară, expoziția gravitează în jurul unor lucrări plasate cu atenție la nivelul ochilor, cu respect pentru ritmul spațiului și în ajutorul privitorul, care transmit relația schimbătoare și adesea contradictorie dintre oameni, orașe și natură, în timp ce inițiază o conversație între lumină și întuneric. Deși subiectul nu este unul nou, inovația vine din modul în care Savu a restabilit credința în dimensiunea picturală, demonstrând încă o dată că există o lume paralelă în spatele tensiunii de suprafață oferite de pânză. De asemenea, expoziția a transmis un grad de intimitate și complicitate între doi vechi prieteni – Șerban Savu și Mihai Pop colaborează încă de la începutul anilor 2000.

Următorul proiect, *Later Edit*, curatoriat de un
istoric de artă local specializat în arta românească
postcomunistă, Maria Orosan-Telea, a adunat un grup
de tineri artiști din Timișoara și Cluj și s-a concentrat
pe procesele pregătitoare din spatele producției
artistice. Proiectul a fost un capitol dintr-o cercetare
curatorială amplă intitulată *Draft*, care a început în
2018. Orosan-Telea a reflectat asupra modului în care
un cumul de idei poate fi modelat de un colectiv de-a
lungul timpului și în contexte neașteptate, analizând
și forma în care experiențele trăite în mod obișnuit
erau percepute de către creatori care lucrează în
diverse medii. Distanța impusă și incertitudinea
derivată din finalizarea proiectului în al doilea val al
pandemiei au testat limitele colaborării artist-curator
și au adăugat o tensiune necesară experimentului.

După o lungă carieră ca designer pentru casele
de modă avangardiste precum Rozalb de Mura și
Patzaikin, Oláh Gyárfás s-a dedicat explorării formei și
materialului. Expoziția *Szénaizmok szalaghegyen /
Mușchi de fân pe munte de panglici* a fost concepută
special pentru Box și își are punctul de plecare în
explorarea mitologiilor și credințelor locale. Inspirat
de metodele de sculptură introduse de Cy Twombly sau
cele specifice curentului Art Deco, Oláh a creat două
creaturi imaginare – *Crocote* și *Leucrocote* – ale căror
nume sunt împrumutate din *Naturalis Historia* a lui
Plinius cel Bătrân. Cele două totemuri poartă o
acumulare de trăsături extraordinare specifice
animalelor domestice. Artistul i-a considerat prieteni și
confidenți personali, protectori ai ideilor nerealizate
și ai viselor suspendate.

Universul sintetic propus de Laurian Popa, un tânăr
artist stabilit în Arad, renumit pentru gruparea
dedicată cercetării noilor media inițiată de *Kinema
Ikon*, a continuat seria dedicată picturii. Alinierea
lucrărilor de largi dimensiuni înfățișând obiecte din
viața de zi cu zi care au fost lipsite de consistență
atât de puternic încât s-au înmuiat, devenind fluide
și spongioase, a fost dublată de o animație care părea
a fi o demonstrație de laborator despre semnificația
conceptului „obiectelor moi".

Dan Vezentan a fost primul artist care a folosit grinda
transversală responsabilă pentru separarea spațiului
în două, ca parte dintr-o instalație – mai precis, grinda
a devenit coloana vertebrală a unui cal uriaș a cărui
formă era sugerată de anvelopele tăiate de la un tractor,
lanțuri, hamuri, șei și ciucuri. Acest cal fantastic a
servit și drept fântână pentru spiritele animalelor
încapsulate în desenele anatomice ale lui Vezentan,
care, în imaginația sa, coborau noaptea să bea din acea
fântână. Expoziția a fost intitulată sugestiv
L' Anatomia del Cavallo, un omagiu adus acestui animal
uimitor care a fost „motorul" înainte de revoluția
industrială. Studiile anatomice ale cailor ne duc înapoi
la finalul Renașterii și debutul manierismului, într-o
încercare a artistului de a sublinia transformarea
socială ireversibilă.

La extrema opusă demonstrației lui Dan Vezentan s-a
aflat proiectul lui Mihai Zgondoiu, *Omul Aproximativ 3.0*.
Zgondoiu a recreat un mediu Sci-Fi purtând urmele
întâlnirilor cu extratereștri, activități paranormale și
ființe din afara acestei lumi, care se unesc în paginile
vechilor cărți de schițe ale artistului și în colecția sa

de reviste. În lumina albastră, cu pupitrele oblice
încărcate cu cataloage de articole despre activități
extraterestre, Box-ul arată ca o navă spațială care se
întoarce dintr-un univers îndepărtat plină cu descoperiri.
Artistul a declarat că proiectul, la care a lucrat în ultimii
cincisprezece ani, nu este despre prezentarea unor
piese de artă izbitoare sau despre răspunsuri, ci mai
degrabă despre generarea unei experiențe diferite, care să
provoace privitorul să exploreze.

Formatul deschis al discursului artistic a fost preluat
de colectivul curatorial KILOBASE BUCHAREST pentru
expozițiile paralele *TRIUMF AMIRIA LOVE LETTER TO
IRINA BUJOR / TRIUMF AMIRIA LOVE LETTER TO MIHAI
MIHALCEA [TRIUMF AMIRIA SCRISOARE DE IUBIRE
CĂTRE IRINA BUJOR / TRIUMF AMIRIA SCRISOARE DE
IUBIRE CĂTRE MIHAI MIHALCEA]*, parte din proiectul de
cercetare de anvergură *TRIUMF AMIRIA* dedicat primei
prezentări instituționale extinse de artă *queer* produsă
în ultimii douăzeci de ani în România. Proiectul,
susținut de Muzeul Național de Artă Contemporană,
a fost găzduit de mai multe instituții din București,
înainte de a migra în alte locații din Europa, sub
forma unor demonstrații artistice mai mici. Cele două
reprezentări din Kunsthalle Bega Box discută despre
procesele conflictuale din spatele definirii identității,
punând în echilibru impactul culturii populare,
performativitatea ca instrument de combatere a
indiferenței sau a disparităților dintre realitate și
lumile personale imaginate.

În ultima parte a anului 2022, pentru expoziția
Ioanei Maria Sisea, *Vremea recoltei*, Box-ul a jucat rolul
unei meta-case. Timp de patru ani, Sisea a

transformat toate obiectele din casa bunicilor
în mărgele. Sute de sfori încărcate cu mărgele
confecționate din diverse materiale – sticlă, metal,
hârtie, material textil, lemn – au fost atârnate de tavan
păstrând configurația casei bătrânești. Conceptul poate
fi interpretat ca un mod de a păstra istoria personală,
dar în același timp, este o contribuție la coagularea
memoriei colective, prin obiectele transformate,
caracteristice unei generații și regiuni specifice.

În ultimii trei ani, Kunsthalle Bega Box a devenit
succesiv un laborator și un spațiu experimental pentru
artiști români tineri sau aflați la mijlocul carierei; aici
au fost prezentate proiecte complexe, care presupun
cercetare și reprezentare și care au implicat publicul
într-o experiență culturală fenomenologică. Pentru
viitor, membrii echipei Kunsthalle Bega își propun
să deschidă Box-ul spre discutarea și accentuarea
limitelor materialității în relație cu specificul
performativ al noilor media.

editare / corectură: Laura Balomiri

[1] Alfred Barr, "Art in Our Time. The Plan of the Exhibition" [„Arta în timpul nostru.
Planul expoziției"], în catalogul expoziției *Art in Our Time* [*Arta în timpul nostru*],
Muzeul de Artă Modernă, New York, 1939, p. 15.

[2] Charlotte Klonk, *Spaces of Experience: Art Gallery Interiors from 1800 to 2000*
[*Spații ale experienței: Interioare de galerie din 1800 până în 2000*], University Press,
Haven & Londra, 2009, p. 218.

[3] Apud *The Hieroglyphics of Space. Reading and experiencing the modern metropolis*
[*Hieroglifele spațiului. Citirea și experimentarea metropolei moderne*], editor Neil Leach,
Routledge, Londra și New York, 2005, p. 143.

[4] Ibidem, p. 17.

Vremea Recoltei
Ioana Maria Sisea

02. 09 – 16. 10. 2022
curatoare: Anca Verona Mihuleț, Iris Ordean

„Bunicii mei aveau o casă, trei paturi, patru mese,
paisprezece scaune, douăzeci și șapte de pahare,
patruzeci și patru de farfurii, trei televizoare, cinci
covoare... Bunicii mei locuiau într-una din cele
patru camere ale casei; celelalte trei erau păstrate
ca o scenografie de care nu ne puteam atinge. Erau
camerele bune la care aveau acces doar oamenii
importanți care veneau în vizită, cum ar fi preoții sau
rudele mai îndepărtate.”

Acesta este un fragment din felul în care Ioana Maria
Sisea își amintește casa bunicilor ei materni. Nu
regăsim urme de nostalgie, dar putem vorbi despre o
responsabilizare a memoriei care deschide calea pentru
înțelegerea poeticii unui spațiu cunoscut în profunzime
de-a lungul unei perioade îndelungate de timp,
atât din perspectiva materiei, cât și din perspectiva
formală. Memoria devine, astfel, aproape un mediu
în sine, esențial pentru potențialul său alegoric în
reprezentarea vizuală a instalației, în organizarea unei
relatări a preocupărilor estetice. Odată cu moartea
bunicilor, relația Ioanei cu casa în care a crescut s-a
transformat. Casa în sine a devenit un construct
spațial încărcat cu straturi de memorie; deposedată
de activitățile zilnice și de tensiunea imediatului,
casa a fost inclusă într-o geografie personală distinct
conturată. Era necesară democratizarea absolută a
spațiului pentru a putea salva memoria locului.

Titlul expoziției, *Vremea recoltei*, este o referire directă
la felul în care toamna, în regiunile mediteraneene
sau în unele zone din sud-estul Europei, legumele și
fructele sunt adesea uscate pe fire de ață și agățate
mai apoi de grinzile din tavan sau de zidurile caselor.
Pentru Ioana, această asociere are o importanță
aparte, fiind o trimitere la activitățile agricole din
jurul casei bunicilor ei, dar și un tribut pentru
procesele care implică muncă fizică, atât în artă,
cât și în viața zilnică. Instalația vorbește despre
intimitatea memoriei trăite examinate sub lupă.
Prin metafora recoltei, ni se facilitează accesul la
universul artistei, informat de experiența subiectivă
a trecutului. Memoria socio-politică face loc instalării
memoriei reflexive care codifică arta atât cognitiv, cât
și emoțional, lăsând loc unei arhive abstractizate, un
loc derridean al începutului și al poruncii.

Există multe moduri în care putem documenta spațiul
privat – ne putem referi la formula cosmologică
propusă de Gaston Bachelard în *Poetica spațiului;* sau
la antagonismul dintre poluare și purificare cercetat
de Mary Douglas încă din anii 1960; sau la cheia de
interpretare structuralistă oferită de Pierre Bourdieu în
studiul caselor Kabyle din Algeria, bazată pe dihotomiile
binare: femeie – bărbat, înăuntru – afară, naștere –
moarte; sau mai recent la teoriile Griseldei Pollock
sau ale lui Jane Rendell despre modernitate și genul
spațiului.

Ioana a eliminat granițele impuse de ziduri și meticulos,
a început să înregistreze și să indexeze toate obiectele
care se găseau în casa bunicilor ei în momentul în care
aceasta a fost moștenită de generația următoare,

cameră cu cameră, obiect cu obiect, material cu
material. Această activitate o transformă pe artistă
într-un arhivist meditativ, lucrând cu memoria
reflexivă, din interior, dar și din afară, asemenea unui
agent. Dispariția utilizatorilor a dus la abstractizarea
acelor posesiuni. Documentarea tradițională a fost
urmată de acțiuni performative menite să ghideze
diviziunea tuturor obiectelor din casă în *mărgele* –
sticla și metalul au fost topite și remodelate în forme
sferice, lemnul a fost traforat în elemente rotunde,
iar materialele textile au fost tăiate manual în
cercuri. Memoria funcționează simultan ca un agent
performativ deconstructiv și reconstructiv – două
fenomene care acționează în același timp, în mod
similar principiului acțiune – reacțiune. Altfel spus,
pe lângă munca afectivă imensă pe care artista a
depus-o în crearea lucrării timp de aproape cinci ani,
se juxtapune o muncă mai practică, de deconstrucție
literală: topirea, tăierea, găurirea, adaptarea tehnicii
de lucru la nevoile fiecărui material. O deconstrucție,
bucată cu bucată, a fostului habitat familial și a
habitusului social, așa cum au fost ele descrise de
Pierre Bourdieu și Zander Navarro, transformând
obiecte care au contribuit formal la experiența
cotidiană trăită, din care a făcut parte foarte des în
copilărie: de la scaune, paturi, covoare, până la aparate
electrocasnice, facturi, căni și pahare. Elemente de
uz cotidian stau alături de *hainele de duminică* sau de
tacâmurile bune.

Deconstrucția este urmată îndeaproape de o abordare
reconstructivă: transformarea conținutului casei
bunicilor în mărgele face parte dintr-o progresie
spațială și o re-producere de sensuri; mărgelele,

proprii reprezentărilor feminine, au devenit codul
de înțelegere a casei. În felul acesta, Ioana Maria
Sisea a identificat casei copilăriei sale cu un univers
eminamente feminin, mobil.

În contextul primei prezentări a proiectului în spațiul
Kunsthalle Bega Box, șiragurile de mărgele sunt
așezate unele lângă celelalte pentru a genera ziduri
penetrabile care descriu amprenta casei bunicilor.
Fiecare zid de mărgele este specific unei camere,
fiind realizat din obiectele divizate care au fost o dată
parte a respectivei încăperi. Foarte puține obiecte au
supraviețuit procesului de transformare, mărturii
ale unui destin anterior, ancorând istoria trecută și
prezentă a instalației.

Filmul care prezintă strângerea obiectelor și
descompunerea mobilierului, alături de două
fotografii din copilăria artistei sunt singurele elemente
ajutătoare care permit audienței să își imagineze
evoluția acelui *locus*, ca și cum privitorul ar fi privit
prin gaura cheii și ar fi surprins imagini rapide ale
unei realități care acum sunt transformate pentru
totdeauna.

Anca Verona Mihuleț, Iris Ordean

TRIUMF AMIRIA LOVE LETTER TO
IRINA BUJOR
TRIUMF AMIRIA LOVE LETTER TO
MIHAI MIHALCEA

10. 06 – 23. 07. 2022
curator: Kilobase Bucharest

În continuarea formatului curatorial „LOVE LETTER
TO [...]", inițiat în 2021 ca parte a conceptualizării
TRIUMF AMIRIA, KILOBASE BUCHAREST și
KUNSTHALLE BEGA au prezentat TRIUMF AMIRIA
LOVE LETTER TO IRINA BUJOR și TRIUMF AMIRIA
LOVE LETTER TO MIHAI MIHALCEA: două expoziții
solo care aduc împreună poziții artistice *queer*, puse
într-un dialog despre posibilitatea de revizitare și
redimensionare continuă a unor lumi care, mai
degrabă decât să fie divergente, sunt suprapuse și se
întrepătrund. Expoziția lui Mihai Mihalcea scoate
la iveală un proces, subtil și intens deopotrivă, de
negociere cu identitățile artistice asumate de-a lungul
timpului, „privirea în secțiune" devenind mobilul
dezvoltării practicii sale artistice. În paralel, expoziția
Irinei Bujor vorbește despre o încercare neobosită de
a-și redefini universul, în care empatia, identitatea,
viitorul sunt investite cu sensuri mereu neașteptate.

Irina Bujor lucrează preponderent în contexte
particulare oferite de orașe mici din România și
Germania. Lucrările sale se bazează pe asocieri
formale care deschid un filon poetic singular;
imaginile și instalațiile cu mai multe straturi
evidențiază fragilitatea și instabilitatea care pun
sub semnul întrebării realitatea noastră aparent

sigură. Aplicând o mare varietate de strategii artistice, Irina dezvoltă o practică multifațetată în jurul unor fenomene obișnuite, care tind să treacă neobservate în subiectele pe care le abordează – râsul, genul, fabricile care produc cultura populară și lucruri care impregnează alte lucruri – totodată instrumentele cu care își recalibrează, constant, universul.

Mihai Mihalcea este artist și coregraf, stabilit în București. A inițiat și co-fondat structuri și proiecte cheie care au dus la recunoașterea internațională a creației românești de dans contemporan. Între 1994-2009 și-a prezentat lucrările coregrafice în instituții din întreaga lume, iar în 2010 și-a asumat o identitate artistică fictivă, Farid Fairuz, sub care și-a continuat activitatea până în 2019, realizând lucrări coregrafice și performance-uri, *live* și pentru cameră, prezentate atât în contextul artelor vizuale cât și al dansului contemporan. Mihai își continuă activitatea la intersecția dintre artele vizuale și dans, păstrând o privire proaspătă asupra propriei deveniri artistice.

Kilobase Bucharest

Omul aproximativ 3.0
Mihai Zgondoiu

08. 04 – 22. 05. 2022

2022: Odiseea spațială
(Întoarcerea Omului aproximativ)

Omul aproximativ 3.0, expoziția lui Mihai Zgondoiu
din Kunsthalle Bega Box, are valoare de manifest
(chiar dacă nu-și propune răspicat asta). Adică, are o
dimensiune programatică și vizionară, comentează
ludic-lucid despre mutațiile curente, dar și despre un
viitor incert, vehiculează imagini bune și de efect,
posedă o retorică provocatoare și e impregnată cu
ironie și spirit critic inteligent. Tema, sau să-i zicem,
miza? Spațiul. Spațiul cosmic, mai exact, cu tot cu
ființele sale din regnuri extraterestre și variile moduri
intelectuale de a le explora; de a dezvălui & interoga &
comenta despre oameni aproximativi (ce-or fi fiind și
aceștia!), dar și despre lumi posibile, acele universuri
pe jumătate reale, pe jumătate închipuite locuite, cum
altfel?, decât de oameni aproximativi.

Sintagma generică trimite, evident, la inconturnabilul
Tristan Tzara, mai exact la al său volum *L'homme*
approximatif, din 1931. Dar titlul expoziției sugerează
în egală măsură ambiguitatea personajelor acestor
universuri nepământești de care ziceam și cu
care lucrează și Mihai Zgondoiu, omul ALIENat,
extraterestrul cu identitate umană aproximativă.
Aceste referințe indică de altfel (două dintre) resursele
principale ale artei lui Mihai Zgondoiu: avangarda
istorică și subcultura paranormalului.

Aici, filonul avangardist se întâlnește cu „studiile"
populare în zona misterelor și a paranormalului,
a lumilor paralele și extraterestre, cu mitologia
personală asumată sarcastic-serios care devin axa
conceptuală și „resursele" acestei expoziții, de fapt.
Interesul artistului pentru această zonă e veche,
cercetarea lui e temeinică. Rezultatul? Materiale
schițate, documente arhivate, imagini făcute,
decupate, apropriate.

Expoziția e gândită instalaționist (și aici se vede
cealaltă calitate a lui Zgondoiu, cea de experimentat
curator), ca un ambient de pe altă lume, dominat
vizual de desenele parietale de mari dimensiuni,
provenite din carnetul de schițe al artistului, executate
în alb pe pereții gri închis, o cartografiere a unei
lumi care (încă) nu există. Printre alte iconuri și
simboluri mai evidente sau mai absconse, regăsim
aici, ca de altfel peste tot în expoziție, acea mască
de extraterestru cu ochii mari și figura alungită,
imaginea simbol a vizitatorilor din alte lumi provenită
din arsenalul științifico-fantastic. Desene și colaje ale
artistului, le regăsim și în montajele video, prezentate
pe ecrane așezate într-o simili-piramidă, un simbol al
puterii creative (a soarelui) și al imortalității, așa cum
probabil este Omul aproximativ al lui Zgondoiu.

Și că pomeneam de prezențe nepământene, artistul
propune o galerie de portrete sub forma unor
fotografii pe plăcuțe de ceramică ovală, precum cele
mortuare, de astă dată dedicate extratereștrilor
dispăruți în filmele lor. Umor și reverență în doze
egale. Tot într-un registru ironic, artistul prezintă
înrămată prima pagină a ziarului american

Roswell Daily Record din 8 iulie 1947 cu știri despre capturarea unei farfurii zburătoare, alături de anunțul căsătoriei Regelui Carol al II-lea în exil, o alăturare, zice artistul, cu semnificații profunde și coincidențe revelatoare despre alienare și destine flotante.

Un loc foarte important în economia acestei lumi aproximative îl ocupă materialul bibliografic, reviste populare și publicații obscure, dedicate lumii OZN-urilor, manifestărilor paranormale, cosmosurilor de circumstanță, ființelor magice și minunilor cvasi-religioase. Acestea sunt adunate în „codexuri" stufoase, adevărate biblii ale domeniului ufologic și paranormal, așezate solemn pe niște pupitre care trimit ambiguu în egală măsură la recuzita bisericească și la cea SF a unei nave spațiale, sugestie accentuată și de ezoterica lumină violet ce îmbracă totul. Ambientul sonor stelar, eteric și misterios învăluie la rândul lui oameni și lucrări.

Nu e întâmplătoare, deci, indicația numerică din titlu, acel „3.0". Aceasta face referire, desigur, la generația următoare a internetului: cea a metaversului, a utilizării descentralizate, a artei inteligenței artificiale, a NFT-ului și a *cloud*-ului. Văzută (și) din această perspectivă, expoziția *Omul aproximativ 3.0* este, vasăzică, un astfel de cloud care vorbește în egală măsură despre actualitatea și mereu actualizabila avangardă și modurile sale de distribuție, dar și despre cele spuse și nespuse privitor la alte universuri, despre noi, despre nori și ființele aproximative care le locuiesc.

Horea Avram

Soft Objects
Laurian Popa

17. 04 – 15. 05. 2021

Soft Objects este o sintagmă care, la prima vedere,
pare una contradictorie în contextul acestui tip de
dialog vizual, dând impresia că ar putea fi vorba
chiar de un oximoron. Obiectele tari, corpurile solide,
își pierd forma și structura, devenind maleabile,
cedând sub efectul unor acțiuni ale căror surse sunt
neclare. Nu este evident ce este acel ceva ce determină
modificarea proprietăților acestor obiecte, care sunt
aceste forțe deformatoare, însă efectul vizual este
evident: obiectele sunt flasce, lipsite de structură
și dezbrăcate de funcția cu care le asociem în mod
normal. Geometria interioară a acestora pare să
lipsească cu desăvârșire, fiind înlocuită de o nouă
organizare internă ce scoate la iveală epuizarea
obiectului ca structură, textură și volum. Vorbim
despre un alt tip de percepție a imaginii a cărei
referință devine ilogică, abstractă, dar care conferă
obiectului o nouă anatomie. Folosind această realitate
modestă a obiectului (*modest body object*) în contextul
actual, putem face o comparație cu societatea, care
devine disfuncțională în anumite conjuncturi.

Avem de-a face cu o asociere de imagini funcțional
- disfuncționale ce conturează o lume fictivă în
care obiectul real este decontextualizat și asociat cu
imaginea *aranjată* a compozițiilor vizuale care se nasc.
Toate aceste *obiecte* devin surse de interpretare vizuală
din care se sustrage culoarea și textura, epuizând
astfel toată esența obiectului pe care o concentrează

într-un alt tip de imagine, care are substanță și în care obiectul-referință este reprezentat fizic, dar care se transformă într-o structură abstractă, neconcretă. Se crează astfel alte repere, alte direcții de citire a imaginii vizuale, care forțează modul de receptare.

Tematica aceasta oferă spațiului, Box-ului Kunsthalle Bega un aer scenografic prin care pictura și animația experimentală se completează, oferind un fir narativ care conturează instalația propusă de mine. Această distopie de naturi statice cuplează privitorul la un alt tip de dialog vizual, prin care se încearcă depășirea blocajelor perceptuale, un dialog care lasă fiecărui privitor șansa de a-și forma propria idee vis-à-vis de lucrare.

Laurian Popa

L' Anatomia del Cavallo
Dan Vezentan

28. 05 – 11. 07. 2021

În primul act, grinda cea mare se transformă într-o coloană vertebrală a unui mamifer, un posibil cal supradimensionat. Apoi apare fântâna: anvelope de tractor, de plug și semănătoare sunt folosite post-mortem într-o cascadă ce compune un nou sistem de hidratare. Înlocuiți de tehnologie în revoluția industrială, patrupezii își revendică acum pământurile. Jgheaburile sintetice stau suspendate în lanțuri și hamuri, fostele mijloace de domesticire și control sunt folosite împotriva tehnologiei, a mașinii.

Vertebrele sunt atent protejate de hamuri și pături moi în așa fel încât spinarea sistemului să fie confortabilă. Caii disecați în cerneală[1] urmează să se adape noaptea, în mod sigur sunetul apei și zurgălăii îi vor atrage hipnotic la sursă. Stația centrală de adăpare se transformă într-o oază pentru animalele de tracțiune, motorul economic are nevoie de reîmprospătare.

Expoziția este un omagiu adus calului, un studiu anatomic al motorului economic, un loc de hidratare pentru animalele de tracțiune.

Dan Vezentan

[1] *Anatomia del cavallo, infermità, et suoi rimedii* de Carlo Ruini (Venezia, 1598). Primul manual de anatomie dedicat unei alte specii decât omul. Reprezintă un punct de reper în publicațiile de specialitate veterinară / cabalină, este cunoscut pentru planșele puternic influențate de lucrările anatomice umane publicate în deceniile anterioare, în special în *De Fabrica Corporis Humani* (Basel, 1543), de Andreas Vesalius.

Szénaizmok szalaghegyen
Mușchi de fân pe munte de panglici
Oláh Gyárfás

27. 11. 2020 – 24. 01. 2021

Unele animale te poartă spre lumea de dincolo.
Lunatice. Tăcute. Psihopompe. Altele păzesc casa, ușa,
intimitatea. Drumul spre sine și drumul spre Dumnezeu,
spre lumea sacră. Domestice, unele animale, îți duc
povara: corpul tău, ceea ce îl încălzește și ceea ce
îl hrănește. Altele sunt jucării de pluș, bibelouri de
porțelan, mici *ready-made*-uri care opresc lacrimile,
înlocuiesc sânul mamei și fac suportabilă lumea
exterioară. Unele se nasc numai din imaginația ta și
numai tu le-ai întâlnit.

Creaturile lui Oláh Gyárfás își petrec timpul prin a
deschide și a închide un univers tranziţional[1]. Un loc
intermediar, «potenţial» cum spune Winnicott, în care
experimentezi autonomia și creativitatea, existenţa
ta particulară. E un loc de joacă și de plăcere, care
te ajută să suporţi rupturile, trecerile, alteritatea și
să compensezi pierderea iluziei unui întreg. Sunt
fantasme arhaice, fioroase, deranjante, paradoxale.

Crocote și *Leucrocote*[2], Szénaizmok și Szalaghegyen[3] au
blană din solzi și organe de fân la vedere; gât, coadă
și piept de lup, spinare de măgar, gură până la urechi
și un os neîntrerupt în loc de dinţi. Au coarne moi
și mobile, ochi la copite, franjuri de capră și labe de
câine. Au piele de războinic pansată cu pânză și ar
putea imita delicat vocea omenească.
Sunt făcute din lemn, pânză de cânepă, făină și

fân, *quoi de plus doux?* (ce ar putea fi mai blând?).
Materialitatea lor te împrietenește imediat cu ele. Sunt
(animale) de casă.

Precum gardianul lui Kafka din nuvela „În fața legii"
– ele au grijă de o poartă. De o singură poartă. De un
prag care e numai al tău. De o promisiune de voiaj.
Ca să treci dincolo, trebuie să redevii copil: să renaști
într-o lume nouă, să ajungi în Korowai.

Pentru Oláh Gyárfás poarta fericirii (care se deschide
singură) trebuie să fie din făină și apă. Ca o pâine.
Poarta trebuie să fie foarte mică, cel care intră este
nevoit să se încline, nu neapărat din umilință, dar ca
simbol al trecerii. În lumea de dincolo trebuie să treci
copil.

Dana Diminescu

[1] D. W. Winnicott, *Transitional Objects and Transitional Phenomena – A Study of the First Not-Me Possession* în: International Journal of Psycho-Analysis, 1953, 34:89-97.

[2] Crocote și Leucrocote sunt *ființe imaginare*, descrise de Ctesias, medicul lui Artaxerxes Mnemon. Borges vorbește despre ele citându-l pe Pliniu (VIII, 3°) în cartea lui tradusă la Editura Polirom, 2006, p. 263.

[3] Szénaizmok și Szalaghegyen, în traducere Mușchi de fân și Munte de panglici.

Later Edit
Gavril Pop
Teo Papadopol
Ana Maria Szöllösi
Nicoló Filippo Rosso
Tijana Kačarević
Lera Kelemen
George Roșu
Adrian Oncu
Dorian Bolca
Miki Velciov
Bogdan Matei
Ioana Terheș
Dreaming About my Unborn Child Group:
Alexandra Satmari, Dona Arnakis,
Elena Langă, Ana Maria Szöllösi,
Oana Sas, Loredana Ilie, Ludmila Naghi,
Maria Ungureanu, Alma Gyovai,
Mihaela Vilău, Gabriela Roșca,
Sânziana Gheorghe, Vivien Fritz

17. 10 – 20. 11. 2020
curator: Maria Orosan-Telea

Later Edit reunește cele treisprezece proiecte cuprinse
în programul curatorial *Draft* desfășurat în Biblioteca
Pavilion pe parcursul a doi ani. Evidențiază o metodă
de cercetare curatorială în care etapele premergătoare
unei expoziții propriu-zise sunt abordate ca momente
stabile și totodată ca elemente ale unui parcurs fluid.

Draft a început în 2018 ca o formă de negociere între
situații artistice în curs de cristalizare și soluțiile de
prezentare pe care acestea le-au adoptat într-un

anumit moment al procesului de producție. Pentru multe dintre proiecte, *Draft* reprezintă contextul potrivit pentru a-și testa funcționalitatea într-o confruntare reală cu publicul sau pentru a genera lucrarea aflată în stadiu de idee cu ajutorul unei intervenții colective și participative.

Later Edit reia toate aceste proiecte într-o etapă ulterioară a existenței lor. Oferă o imagine simultană, într-un spațiu comun, a lucrărilor acumulate în timp în jurul conceptului de a prezenta idei artistice într-o formă vizuală cu statut intermediar și incert.

DRAFT (draftcuratorialprogram.ro) este un program curatorial care prezintă proiecte artistice în stadiu de idee, proiecte parțial realizate sau eșantioane replicabile la scară mai mare. Conceptualizarea, cercetarea și analiza sunt punctele de reper în identificarea formatului potrivit pentru expunerea acestora. Astfel că, prezentarea ideilor în stadiul lor intermediar devine un demers comprehensiv în sine și chestionează relația dintre procesul de creație și opera finită. Limitele vagi dintre acestea sunt dislocate tocmai prin intenția de a face un stop cadru într-o structură conceptuală aflată în derulare.

Interacțiunea cu publicul devine premisă generativă și poate avea un rol determinant în creșterea sau deturnarea traiectoriei viitorului proiect. Privilegiind conceptele cumulative hrănite de comunicarea interumană directă, ne propunem să creăm un context al proximității și al discuțiilor libere, în care emițătorul și receptorul să-și schimbe în permanență rolurile.

Maria Orosan-Telea

Echinocțiu
Șerban Savu

20. 03 – 20. 05. 2020
expoziție îngrijită de Mihai Pop

Preambul.
Un inocent joc de societate, la cumpăna dintre ani,
mi-a arătat ce îmi este destinat anul acesta: dificilul
moment al bătăliei dintre noapte și zi, punctul de
fragilitate maximă în care se confruntă forțele naturii.
În dreptul alegerii mele, cartea de joc povestește că,
într-o astfel de zi, în China, oamenii stau în casă, la
adăpost de demonii calendarului, atât de puternice
și înfricoșătoare sunt energiile duale ale naturii în
momentul Echinocțiului de primăvară.

Penumbra. Pictura.
Există o dimensiune latentă în pictura lui Șerban
Savu, întotdeauna prezentă, dar niciodată clarificată,
nici măcar în interviurile pe care le-a dat artistul
de-a lungul anilor. Iar scoaterea ei la lumină
implică o privire perseverentă, eliberată de căutarea
anecdoticului, dar și de reperele istoriei artelor (într-un
cuvânt, dezactivarea cunoștințelor despre opera lui
Savu). Acest exercițiu cere cercetarea atentă a pânzei,
din nou și din nou, și fixarea privirii în penumbră,
pe suprafețele „reziduale" ale imaginii, întotdeauna
aflate acolo ca balans necesar al subiectului pictat.
Personajele lui Savu aparțin și ele penumbrei,
suspendate la rândul lor, continuu, într-un spațiu
încărcat de potențialitatea unei acțiuni, dar aflat încă
în adormire, în așteptarea de dinaintea declanșării
„realității". Aceste personaje sunt mai degrabă

definite prin relația cu fluxul naturii (hibernare,
așteptare, germinare), decât prin rolul lor în „tabloul
social" (și, prin extensie, în economia lucrării). Chiar
dacă natura pictată de Savu este de cele mai multe
ori artificială, subsumată arhitecturii și adaptată
personajelor, relația natură – om e subiectul lăuntric
al picturilor lui, niciodată spus, scris, descris. Această
relație de interdependență este umanitatea pe care
pictura lui o poartă latent în ea.

Pictura. Expoziția.
Ce poate face cel mai bine pictura? În cazul nostru,
să mențină intact echilibrul fragil al părților. Și ne
vom regăsi în ea doar în măsura în care se oglindește
ambiguitatea acestei tensiuni, departe de falsul
certitudinilor simplificatoare. De aceea continuăm să
o privim, căci conține obscuritatea atât de importantă,
compostul care ne hrănește. Picturile poartă în ele
penumbra, iar expoziția ca întreg este la rândul ei
purtătoarea unei incertitudini fertile. Văzută astfel,
expoziția devine antidotul motorului mercantil al
supra-producției scenei de artă actuale. Încă un motiv
pentru a o vernisa în momentul Echinocțiului de
primăvară. Astfel, pictura-purtătoare-de-penumbră
capătă claritate, arătându-se în cel mai potrivit
moment, datorită capacității noastre de a privi
cu atenție în zona de semiobscuritate a tabloului.
Trecerea de la „iarnă" la „primăvară" se face în artă
prin acest proces anevoios, concentrat, al privirii.

Expoziția. Umbra.
Până la Echinocțiul de primăvară, când, pe 20
martie, pictura și receptarea ei în expoziție capătă
drepturi egale, tentația discursivă este de a echivala

construcția expoziției cu drumul de la întunericul germinativ la lumină. Punctul de echilibru perfect între zi și noapte marchează starea de excepționalitate a mediului reflexiv pe care expoziția îl creează. Acest lucru este posibil pentru că Șerban Savu își asumă natural folosirea metaforei în creația sa. Ni s-a părut, astfel, firesc să numim și să deschidem expoziția de Echinocțiu.

Addenda.
În anii studenției, călătoream în fiecare primăvară din Clujul încă gri, mohorât, la Student Fest-ul timișorean, care deborda de vitalitate. Totul era deschidere și înnoire. Și totuși, expoziția pe care o construiam împreună de fiecare dată, în primăvara care dădea pe dinafară, era invariabil cu și despre partea întunecată a fiecăruia dintre noi. O stare fragilă și fertilă deopotrivă, păstrând – indiferent de practica fiecăruia – melancolia și umbra.

Mihai Pop

Cristian Rusu, *Ghost Geometry,* 2022
curator Diana Marincu
Kunsthalle Bega
exhibition view

next spread

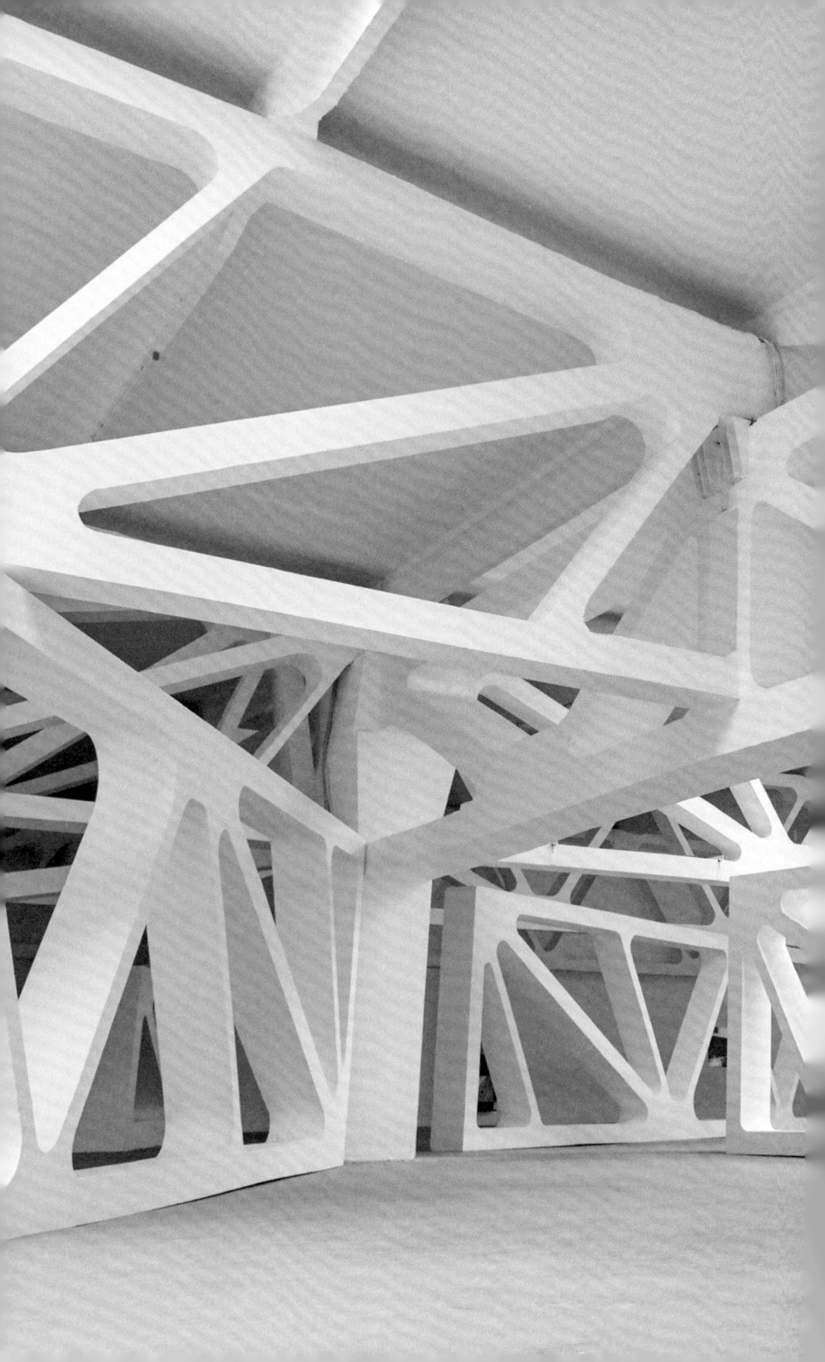

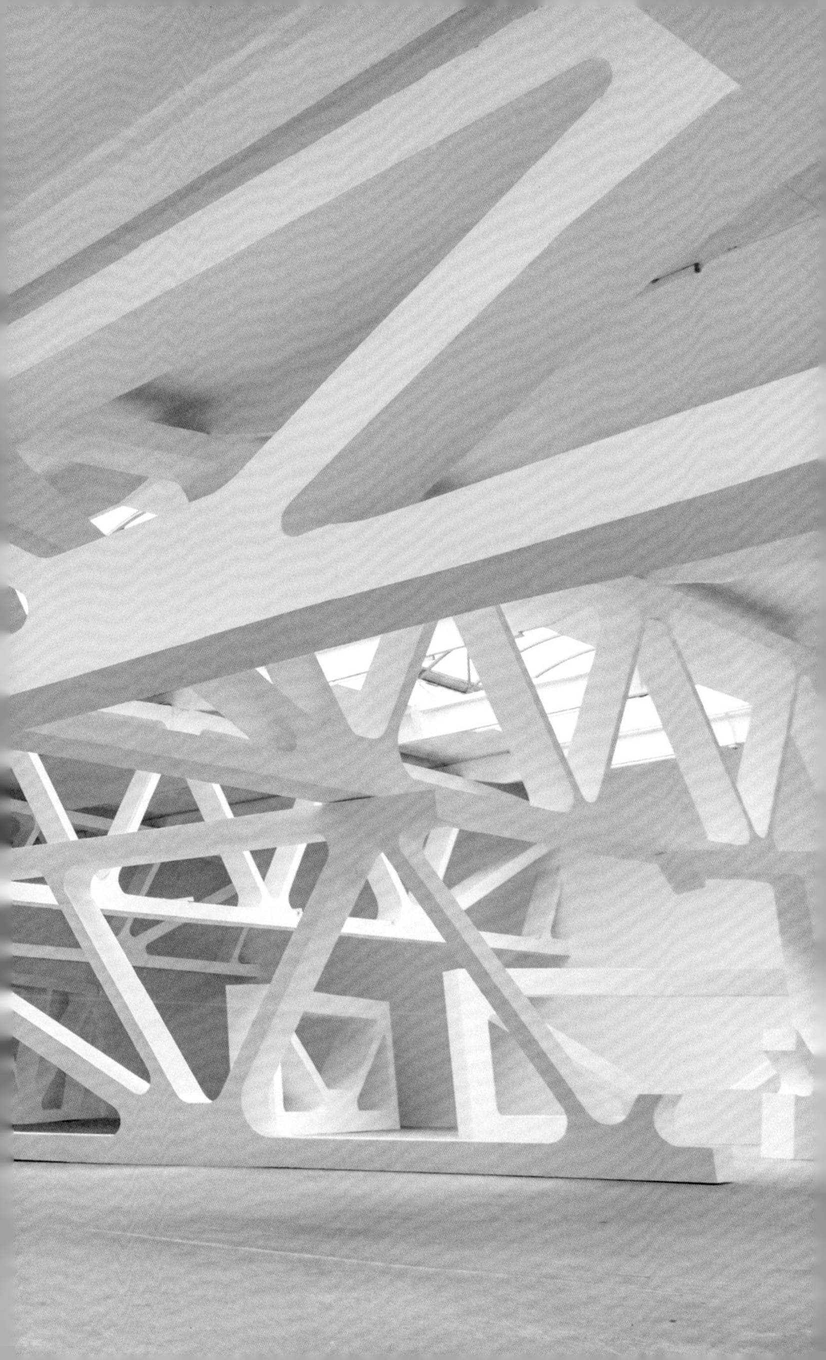

This publication is released to accompany the project:
Kunsthalle Bega School – space for creative and educational projects (second edition, 2022)

Editors: Alina Cristescu, Anca Verona Mihuleț,
Bogdan Rața

Project manager: Andreea Drăghicescu

Design: Kunsthalle Bega

Texts: Horea Avram, Dana Diminescu, Kilobase Bucharest, Anca Verona Mihuleț, Iris Ordean, Maria Orosan-Telea, Mihai Pop, Laurian Popa, Dan Vezentan

Photos: Vlad Cîndea, Adrian Oncu, Flavius Neamciuc, Șerban Savu © Courtesy the artist and Plan B Cluj, Berlin, Dan Vezentan, Mihai Zgondoiu

Translations: Anca Verona Mihuleț, Iris Ordean,
Rita Tasi, Andreea Tiriplică

Project management, Kerber Verlag: Lydia Fuchs

Production, Kerber Verlag: Jens Bartneck

Printed and published by
Kerber Verlag
Windelsbleicher Str. 166–170
33659 Bielefeld
Germany
+49 521 950 08 10
+49 521 950 08 88 (F)
info@kerberverlag.com
kerberverlag.com

Kerber publications are distributed worldwide:

ACC Art Books
Sandy Lane
Old Martlesham
Woodbridge, IP12 4SD
UK
+44 1394 38 99 50
+44 1394 38 99 99 (F)
accartbooks.com
uksales@accartbooks.com

Artbook | D.A.P.
75 Broad Street, Suite 630
New York, NY 10004
USA
+1 (212) 627-1999
+1 (212) 627-9484 (F)
artbook.com
orders@dapinc.com

AVA Verlagsauslieferung AG
Centralweg 16
8910 Affoltern am Albis
Switzerland
+41 44 762 42 50
+41 44 762 42 10 (F)
avainfo@ava.ch

Zeitfracht GmbH
Verlagsauslieferung
+49 711 7860 2254
bestellung@zeitfracht.de

The Deutsche Nationalbibliothek lists this publication
in the Deutsche Nationalbibliografie: dnb.de.

ISBN 978-3-7356-0908-3
www.kerberverlag.com
Printed in Germany

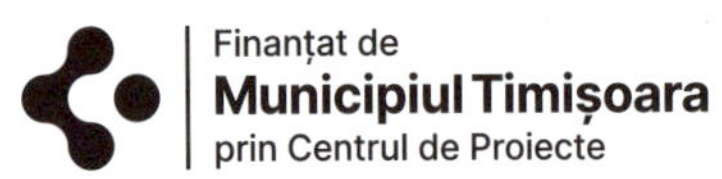

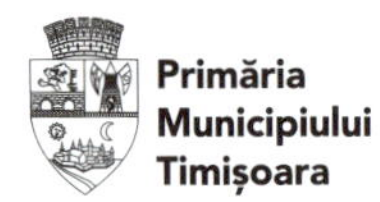

Project co-funded by Primăria Municipiului Timișoara, through Centrul de Proiecte Timișoara, under the priority program "Repere în cultură"

Proiect co-finanțat de Primăria Municipiului Timișoara prin Centrul de Proiecte al Municipiului Timișoara în cadrul programului prioritar „Repere în cultură"

sponsori / sponsors

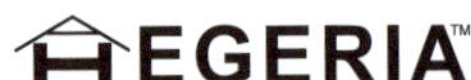

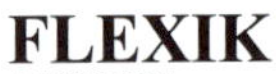

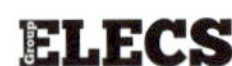

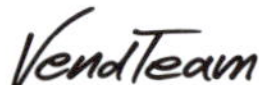

parteneri / partners

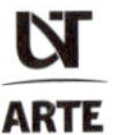

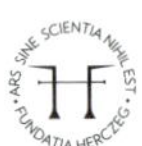

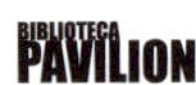

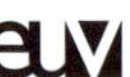

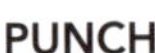

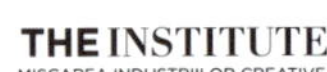

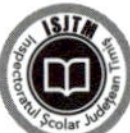

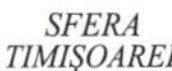

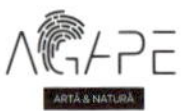

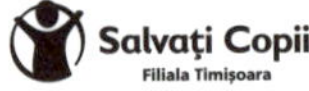

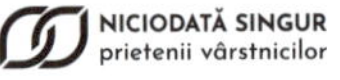

parteneri media / media partners

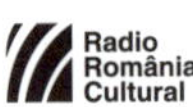

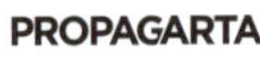

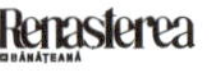

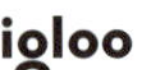

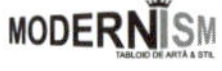

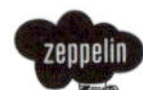

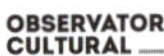

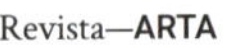

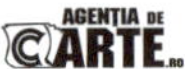

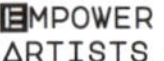

Kunsthalle Bega
Circumvalațiunii 10
Timișoara (RO)
kunsthallebega.ro